MIHIR BHAGWAT

BEYOND BORDERS

BlueRose ONE .com
Stories Matter
NewDelhi • London

BLUEROSE PUBLISHERS
India | U.K.

For permissions requests or inquiries regarding this publication, please contact:

BLUEROSE PUBLISHERS
www.BlueRoseONE.com
info@bluerosepublishers.com
+91 8882 898 898
+4407342408967

ISBN: 978-93-7018-848-8

Cover design: Yash Singhal
Typesetting: Namrata Saini

First Edition: June 2025

Acknowledgements

I begin by expressing my deepest gratitude to my parents. Their unwavering support, patience, and belief in my vision have been the bedrock of this entire endeavor. Their encouragement gave me the strength and focus to see Beyond Borders through to completion.

My sincere thanks go to the BlueRose team for their exceptional dedication and professionalism. Their expertise in editing, design, and publication transformed this manuscript into a polished and impactful work.

Special appreciation is owed to my teacher Shri/Mr. Utsab Banerjee, whose insightful mentorship and constructive guidance have been Extremely valuable in shaping the direction and depth of this book.

I am also grateful to my mentors, teachers, friends whose critical feedback, knowledge, and encouragement have enriched the research and clarity of this project.

Finally, I acknowledge the diplomats, scholars, and thinkers whose works and experiences inspired the themes explored in this book.

To all who contributed – directly or indirectly – thank you for being part of this journey.

Preface

In a world marked by division, conflict, and often chaos, **diplomacy** emerges as the **silent force** that holds the key to lasting peace. This book, ***Beyond Borders***, seeks to remind us that **diplomacy** is not just a tool of power or strategy; it is a pathway to harmony, understanding, and a shared future. From the ancient wisdom of the **Artha Shastra** to the timeless vision of **Vasudhaiva Kutumbakam** – the idea that "the world is one family" – India's diplomatic journey has been one of bridging divides, building connections, and fostering **mutual respect** among nations. In a time where the world is more interconnected yet seemingly more fractured, India stands as a beacon of what can be achieved when diplomacy is not about domination, but about **dialogue** and **mutual growth**.

The world has seen its share of wars, ideological battles, and geopolitical struggles. **India's unique position in global affairs, however,** has always been different. It has consistently refused to be drawn into conflicts that serve only to deepen divides. Instead, India has championed the cause of **peace, stability, and collaboration**. It has quietly and determinedly shown the world that diplomacy is the **true strength of nations**, not military might. Diplomacy is more than just negotiations at the highest levels of government. This book takes you through the rich tapestry of **India's diplomatic legacy**, its **non-alignment movement**, and how India has navigated through centuries of complex international relations with one simple belief – **peace is the ultimate form**

of power. It is this vision of **"One Earth, One Family, One Future"** that India has carried forward in its diplomatic ethos. It is this belief that drives its foreign policy today, even as we face challenges on the global stage. For **India, diplomacy** is not just about balancing power; it is about creating bridges across cultures, nations, and people.

India is rightly referred to as the Golden Bird, a symbol of immense wealth, prosperity, and cultural brilliance. To protect this treasure, the divine has granted India remarkable natural defenses. The towering **Himalayas** stand to the **North**, guarding the country with their majestic presence. To the **South**, the vast expanse of the **Indian Ocean** shields the land while offering opportunities for maritime trade. In the **East**, the **Bay of Bengal** acts as both a barrier and a gateway, protecting India's shores. To the **West**, the **Thar Desert** forms a natural fortress, keeping the land safe. Together, these geographic features serve as the protective embrace for the Golden Bird, ensuring its safety and fostering its growth.

Let this book inspire you to believe that **peace is possible**— and that diplomacy is the way to bring it about. Because in the end, **diplomacy is not just a career; it is a calling. It is the path that leads us from confrontation to cooperation, from fear to understanding, from division to unity.**

What is Diplomacy?

"Diplomacy is the heartbeat of peace, turning a world of conflict into a paradise where every life is cherished, and harmony reigns."

\- *Mihir Bhagwat*

Contents

Introduction

India has never needed to conquer to lead. Her power lies not in force, but in values – in the wisdom of her sages, the courage of her freedom fighters, and the vision of unity she carries to the world stage. From ancient times to modern challenges, India has stood as a voice of reason, a messenger of peace, and a guardian of dignity. This is not just diplomacy,this is India's spirit in action. A spirit that chooses humanity over hatred, dialogue over destruction, and peace over pride.

When India speaks, it's for the world;
when India acts, it's for the people."

"Peace is not a privilege, it's a right –
India defends it for all."

CHAPTER 1

Foundations of Indian Diplomacy

Diplomatic Tradition of India

India's diplomatic tradition is not a product of recent history—it is a continuum that dates back to ancient times, enriched by philosophy, strategy, and a deep understanding of cultural coexistence. From the wisdom of Kautilya's *Artha Shastra* to the principles enshrined in the Indian Constitution, the foundations of Indian diplomacy rest on a blend of civilizational values and pragmatic statecraft. This chapter traces the origins, evolution, and guiding principles that form the bedrock of Indian diplomacy.

India's diplomatic thought can be traced to ancient texts like the *Mahabharata, Ramayana,* and especially Kautilya's *Artha Shastra*. These works laid down strategic frameworks for negotiation, alliances, and conflict resolution.

Kautilya's Artha Shastra emphasised *realpolitik,* advocating for state interest as the highest goal. He categorised neighboring states into natural enemies and allies and advised rulers on espionage, treaties, and the balance of power. The concept of *Rajamandala* (circle of states) laid the groundwork for understanding geopolitics and the fluidity of international relations.

At the same time, ancient Indian diplomacy was also guided by *dharma* (ethical conduct), illustrating the balance between pragmatism and moral responsibility. India's soft power—long before the term was coined—has historically flowed through trade, religion, and culture. The spread of Buddhism across Asia, especially under Emperor Ashoka, exemplifies the use of moral and cultural influence as diplomatic tools. Indian merchants, scholars, and monks created bridges with Southeast

Asia, Central Asia, and even the Mediterranean. These peaceful exchanges laid the foundation for mutual respect, which continues to shape India's approach to foreign relations today. India's diplomacy stands on centuries-old foundations of moral reasoning, cultural pluralism, and pragmatic statecraft. In every phase of its evolution, from Kautilya to Nehru, from Ashoka's edicts to contemporary global negotiations, Indian diplomacy has sought to harmonise power with purpose.

As the 21st century unfolds, these foundations provide not just a legacy but a compass for India's global journey.

India's diplomacy is a dynamic blend of ancient wisdom and modern vision. It is shaped not just by geopolitical imperatives but also by civilizational ethos and moral principles. As India's global role expands in the 21st century, these foundational elements provide both stability and direction.

The next chapters will explore how these enduring principles are applied in practice through India's relationships with its neighbors, major powers, and multilateral forums.

It's widely acknowledged that India, or Bharat, is a peaceful nation. However, our choice not to engage in petty matters is a testament to our strength, not a sign of weakness.

The rise of Indian diplomacy began many centuries ago, long before modern India existed. One of the earliest thinkers of diplomacy was **Chanakya**, also known as **Kautilya**, who lived around 2,300 years ago. He was the advisor to Emperor Chandragupta Maurya and wrote the famous book called the *Artha Shastra*. In this book, he explained how a king should deal with other kingdoms through smart planning, strong alliances, and sometimes, if required, even spying. He believed that a ruler must protect the country's interests by using both power and wisdom. This was one of the first examples of Indian diplomacy.

Later, in the 3rd century BCE, **Emperor Ashoka** became an pivotal figure in Indian diplomatic history. After seeing the destruction caused by war, he chose a different path. He renounced violence, instead promoting peace and kindness. He sent messages and Buddhist monks to other countries to spread the ideas of non-violence and compassion. This was a form of cultural diplomacy—building friendships through shared values, not force.

As time went on, India continued to interact with other countries, especially through trade and culture. Indian goods, art, and religions like Buddhism and Hinduism reached Southeast Asia, Central Asia, and beyond. Even when India was ruled by foreign powers during the medieval and colonial periods, the idea of peaceful exchange and mutual respect remained strong.

The foundations of Indian diplomacy stretch across more than two millennia, far deeper than the establishment of modern institutions. India's diplomatic spirit was not born in the embassies of New Delhi, but in the royal courts of ancient emperors, the wisdom of philosophical texts, and the cultural bridges built by monks, scholars, and kings. Indian diplomacy has never been a singular tactic of governance; it is a civilizational force, shaped by a constant dialogue between power and principle, conquest and cooperation, realism and righteousness.

The journey begins in the **ancient period**, with the **Mauryan Empire**, founded by **Chandragupta Maurya** in the 4th century BCE. Under the guidance of his prime minister and mentor **Chanakya**, also known as **Kautilya**, the Mauryas developed one of the earliest and most sophisticated models of diplomacy. Kautilya's *Artha Shastra* is a text of stunning clarity and pragmatism, laying out detailed principles of foreign policy, alliances, espionage, and interstate relations. Unlike Western doctrines developed centuries later, Kautilya's vision was unapologetically strategic yet deeply Indian—one that saw the balance of power, deterrence, and calculated peace as a tool for long-term stability. His approach to diplomacy was not just theoretical; it was applied. Chandragupta maintained ties with Hellenistic rulers, including **Seleucus I**, and their treaty included diplomatic exchanges and even a Greek ambassador at the Mauryan court—evidence of early Indo-Greek engagement.

The diplomatic legacy continued with **Emperor Ashoka**, one of India's most influential rulers. After the devastating **Kalinga War**, Ashoka transformed into a peace-seeking monarch who used diplomacy not for expansion but for moral outreach. He dispatched emissaries across Asia—Sri Lanka, Egypt, Syria, and beyond—not with swords but with messages of **dhamma** (righteous conduct).

These envoys carried not only the ideas of Buddhism but also India's civilizational identity: one that respected peace, coexistence, and the power of persuasion over violence. His rock edicts are among the earliest recorded instances of a ruler openly appealing to international morality, long before the idea of universal human values was debated in global assemblies.

As the Mauryan Empire faded, the mantle of leadership passed to the **Gupta Empire** in the 4th century CE. Often hailed as India's **Golden Age**, this period saw diplomacy evolve alongside cultural and scientific flourishing. **Samudragupta**, the empire's most prominent military leader, combined military success with an astute diplomatic strategy. The famous **Allahabad Pillar Inscription** describes how he accepted tributes and maintained relations with foreign and frontier rulers, allowing them to govern autonomously in exchange for allegiance. His policies reflected a shrewd understanding of soft power and political realism. During the Gupta period, India also emerged as a cultural superpower. Buddhist scholars, mathematicians, and poets travelled abroad, while foreign travellers such as **Fa-Hien** visited India, drawn by its knowledge systems and religious institutions. Diplomacy during this era was not only about treaties—it was about knowledge-sharing, artistic exchange, and the quiet expansion of influence through learning and culture.

The decline of classical empires gave way to the **medieval era**, a time marked by regional kingdoms and greater interaction with the West and Central Asia. India was far from isolated, remaining an active participant in the international sphere. The **Chola Empire** in southern India, particularly under **Rajaraja Chola** and **Rajendra Chola**, exemplified maritime diplomacy at its peak. The Cholas sent naval expeditions and diplomatic missions to **Southeast Asia**, including present-day Thailand, Cambodia, and Indonesia. They engaged with China's Song Dynasty and maintained trade and cultural ties across the Bay of Bengal. This early form of Indo-Pacific diplomacy showcased India's reach long before modern strategic terms defined the region.

In North India, the emergence of the **Delhi Sultanate** and later the **Mughal Empire** introduced new layers to Indian diplomacy. These regimes interacted not just with local kingdoms but also with the great powers of Central Asia, the Middle East, and Europe. **Akbar the Great** was not only a military leader but a philosopher-king who believed in **Sulh-i-Kul**—universal peace. His policy of religious tolerance was itself a diplomatic doctrine that fostered internal harmony while projecting a model of inclusive governance to the world. Akbar's court welcomed Jesuit missionaries, Persian scholars, and ambassadors from various lands. The **Mughals**, especially under **Jahangir** and **Shah Jahan**, maintained a sophisticated court protocol, sent and received envoys, and negotiated trade and political treaties with the British, the Portuguese, and the Ottoman Empire. These interactions were formal and strategic, showing that even medieval India had a global footprint in diplomacy, trade, and culture.

As power shifted in later centuries, the **Marathas** and **Sikhs** engaged in complex negotiations with both Indian and European powers. The **Maratha Confederacy**, despite its fragmented structure, conducted diplomacy to protect interests and build coalitions, often negotiating with the British East India Company, Mysore, and the remnants of the Mughals. **Ranjit Singh**, the Sikh emperor of Punjab, famously maintained cordial relations with the British and forged alliances that preserved his autonomy longer than most Indian kingdoms. These leaders did not merely react to foreign powers; they shaped regional diplomacy with courage, clarity, and calculation.

However, the **advent of colonial rule** under the British dramatically altered India's diplomatic autonomy. Indian voices were muted in global affairs, and foreign policy decisions were made in London. But the Indian spirit was not extinguished. Cultural diplomacy continued, now in new forms. **Swami Vivekananda's** electrifying speech in Chicago in 1893 reintroduced India to the West, not as a colonised land, but as a cradle of timeless wisdom. **Rabindranath Tagore** travelled across continents, advocating for dialogue between civilisations, and warning against aggressive nationalism. These thinkers were not government diplomats, but their words carried the weight of India's conscience. Meanwhile, **Mahatma Gandhi** revolutionised political strategy with nonviolence as a global moral message. His movements influenced civil rights leaders in America and freedom struggles in Africa, turning India's freedom struggle into an instrument of international diplomacy.

Bharat's Sangram Against British Samrajya: Freedom Through Diplomacy

The quest for India's independence was not only a battle fought on the streets but also on the global stage. Indian leaders, through diplomatic means, mobilized support, negotiated with colonial powers, and strategically positioned India's struggle for freedom as a moral cause that resonated internationally. Diplomacy, in this sense, was not just a tool of negotiation but a means to shape global opinion, garner allies, and expose the injustices of colonial rule.

At the forefront of this diplomatic effort was **Mahatma Gandhi**, whose leadership transcended traditional political methods. Gandhi's philosophy of non-violence was not merely a domestic policy; it was a diplomatic strategy that positioned India's fight for independence as a moral struggle on the world stage. His **Salt March** and subsequent **Civil Disobedience Movement** captured global attention and put pressure on the British Empire. Gandhi's diplomatic efforts reached beyond the borders of India, attracting the sympathy of other colonised nations and gaining support from international figures. By the time of the **Gandhi-Irwin Pact** in 1931, India's struggle for freedom was no longer seen as a local rebellion, but as part of a global conversation about self-determination and human rights.

The Indian National Congress, under Gandhi's leadership, was not only focused on internal resistance but was also engaged in a diplomatic effort to forge **international alliances** and shape global sentiment. While the leaders of the Congress continued to negotiate with the British government through formal channels, they also worked to **mobilise the international community** by highlighting the hypocrisy of colonial rule. Indian leaders consistently emphasised that their fight was not merely for political independence, but for the right to self-governance, equality, and dignity. Through persistent engagement, the Congress was able to garner international sympathy, especially as other countries around the world began to reject imperialism.

India's diplomatic efforts took on a more structured form as it engaged directly with European powers. The **Round Table Conferences** in London during the early 1930s were a key example of how India used diplomatic negotiations to demand greater autonomy from Britain. Gandhi's presence at these conferences, despite the difficulties in reaching agreements, showed the world that India was serious about its independence and that its leaders were capable of engaging on par with other world powers. Although the conferences ultimately did not yield immediate results, they showcased India's ability to assert itself diplomatically, compelling Britain to take India's demands seriously.

Another important avenue for Indian diplomacy was the **League of Nations**, where India began to press its case for independence on an international scale. Indian leaders, especially **Jawaharlal Nehru**, began to develop relationships with other global leaders and countries sympathetic to the cause of self-determination. They argued not just for India's independence but for the broader rights of colonised nations, gaining the attention of emerging global powers and establishing India as a vocal advocate for the rights of oppressed peoples worldwide.

The outbreak of **World War II** in 1939 created a new dynamic in India's diplomatic strategy. Britain, embroiled in the war, sought India's support, but Indian leaders saw this as an opportunity to press for greater concessions. With Gandhi leading the charge for non-cooperation and Nehru advocating for more radical measures, India's struggle for independence gained further international recognition. India's refusal to support the war effort without a promise of independence highlighted the deepening divide between Britain and its colony. During this time, the **Indian National Army (INA)**, led by **Subhas Chandra Bose**, became a distinct and significant factor. Bose's efforts to seek support from **Axis powers** like Nazi Germany and Imperial Japan were a controversial yet bold attempt to use international diplomacy to break the shackles of colonialism. While their strategies for achieving independence differed significantly, both Bose and Gandhi, through their distinct diplomatic approaches, amplified India's demand for freedom on the world stage.

The fate of Subhas Chandra Bose after August 1945 is a subject that sparks a lot of discussion. Most people think he either vanished or passed away shortly after the war wrapped up, which suggests he probably didn't stray far from Gandhi's philosophy in any meaningful way after WWII. This idea definitely has its shortcomings, especially when it comes to timing and the facts. In truth, Bose started to drift away from Gandhi's principles well before and during the war, which is clear from his creation of the Forward Bloc and his choice to seek assistance from Axis powers. I'd recommend removing this sentence, as it misrepresents both the facts and the timeline. His change in strategy was noticeable much earlier and persisted throughout the war. However, both Gandhi and Bose shared profound mutual respect.

In this period, the **Indian diaspora** also played a key diplomatic role. Across the world, Indian leaders and activists, including figures like **Lala Lajpat Rai**, **Gopal Krishna Gokhale**, and **Dadabhai Naoroji**, worked tirelessly to gain support from foreign governments, intellectuals, and political leaders. They campaigned to raise awareness of the oppressive policies of the British Empire, shaping a global narrative in which India's struggle for freedom became emblematic of the broader fight against colonialism.

The outbreak of **World War II** in 1939 brought about a significant shift in the dynamics of India's independence movement. The war placed Britain in a vulnerable position, draining its resources and weakening its global influence. India's leaders, especially Gandhi and Nehru, seized this opportunity to push for independence. The **Quit India Movement of 1942** became not only a cry for immediate freedom but also a **strategic diplomatic message** to the British

Empire. The world was watching, and India's demand for freedom was gaining unparalleled traction.

And so, after decades of sacrifice, negotiation, and relentless pursuit—through marches and meetings, protests and pacts—**India stood tall as an independent nation on the dawn of 15th August 1947**. The Union Jack was lowered, and the **Tiranga** rose high, fluttering not just as a flag, but as a symbol of **hard-earned sovereignty**. This was not merely the end of colonial rule; it was the triumph of diplomacy, determination, and the indomitable spirit of a civilisation that had waited centuries to reclaim its voice. **Bharat was free, proud, peaceful, and ready to speak for itself on the world stage.**

Jawaharlal Nehru became India's first Prime Minister, giving Indian diplomacy a clear direction. He believed that India should stay independent in world politics and not take sides in the Cold War between the USA and USSR. He promoted peace, respect for international laws, and cooperation with other countries. He also helped build strong diplomatic institutions

Meanwhile, **India's engagement with international organisations**, particularly the **League of Nations** and later the **United Nations**, demonstrated India's diplomatic maturity. Indian leaders, especially Nehru, articulated the case for Indian self-rule in global forums, gaining the **sympathy of newly independent countries** and global powerhouses that had begun to understand the injustices of colonialism. The growing **global movement towards decolonisation** became an essential backdrop for India's independence, and India's diplomatic struggle was intrinsically linked to the wider fight for freedom taking place around the world.

From Chanakya's clever strategies to Nehru's peaceful and independent approach, Indian diplomacy grew from ancient wisdom into a modern and respected voice in world affairs.

From Battlefields to UN Floors: The Kashmir Question Begins

In the twilight months of 1947, as the wounds of Partition were still raw and borders freshly drawn, the newly independent nations of India and Pakistan found themselves entangled in their first armed conflict. At the heart of this confrontation lay the princely state of Jammu and Kashmir — a region of strategic and symbolic importance.

Maharaja Hari Singh, the ruler of Kashmir, had hoped to remain independent. But as tribal militias from Pakistan, supported by Pakistani forces, invaded the state in October 1947, Maharaja Hari Singh was compelled to seek help from India. On October 26, 1947, he signed the Instrument of Accession, formally joining India. The very next day, Indian troops were airlifted into Kashmir to repel the invasion. Thus began the first Indo-Pak war—a conflict that would not only define the future of Kashmir but also set the stage for India's early engagement with global diplomacy.

As the conflict escalated and fears of a larger war loomed, India chose the path of international dialogue. On January 1, 1948, the Indian government approached the United Nations, invoking Article 35 of the UN Charter. It was a bold diplomatic move—not a sign of weakness, but of faith in multilateralism and global justice.

The United Nations responded by establishing the United Nations Commission for India and Pakistan (UNCIP). Its mission was to investigate the situation and work towards a peaceful resolution. In April 1948, the Security Council passed Resolution 47, which called for an immediate ceasefire, the withdrawal of Pakistani-backed forces from Kashmir, and a subsequent reduction of Indian forces. Once peace was restored, a plebiscite was to be held to determine the will of the people of Kashmir.

The ceasefire was eventually achieved on January 1, 1949, bringing a temporary halt to open hostilities. However, the conditions laid out by the UN—particularly the demilitarisation of the region and the holding of a plebiscite—were never fully implemented. Differing interpretations and a lack of trust between the two nations kept the matter unresolved, and the Kashmir dispute was born.

For India, the war was more than a territorial defense—it was a test of its sovereignty, its ideals, and its diplomatic maturity. Turning to the United Nations reflected a deep commitment to peaceful dialogue in a moment of national crisis. It also established India's early role as a responsible voice on the world stage—one that preferred resolution over retaliation, and reason over rage.

The 1947- 48 war may have ended with a line drawn across Kashmir, but it also etched India's presence into the evolving narrative of international diplomacy. The echoes of that war—and the questions it raised—continue to shape geopolitical discourse even today.

The end of the 1947–48 war did not mark a resolution—it marked a fracture. What had begun as an invasion by tribal militias and escalated into a full-blown war between two newly independent nations ultimately led to the drawing of an uneasy line: the ceasefire line, later known as the Line of Control. This line did not just divide territory; it carved through identity, memory, and geopolitics. Jammu and Kashmir, once princely and undecided, was now split between two sovereign states, each asserting rightful ownership, each building a narrative of legitimacy.

The war, while brief, cast a long shadow. It gave birth to a conflict that would become deeply embedded in the psyche of both India and Pakistan. In India, the war was seen as the first true test of its sovereignty and diplomatic vision. Its decision to approach the United Nations—an act that required a rare mix of confidence and restraint—was rooted in a desire to be seen not just as a regional power, but as a responsible member of the international community. Yet, while India saw its accession of Kashmir as complete and constitutional, Pakistan viewed it as premature and disputed, a disagreement that hardened over time.

The involvement of the United Nations created initial hope but eventually led to diplomatic stagnation. The promise of a plebiscite, outlined in UN Resolution 47, faded as ground realities outpaced global idealism. The conditions laid out in the resolution—beginning with Pakistan's withdrawal of forces—were never fulfilled, and over time, the international community grew weary of the stalemate. What remained was a frozen conflict, periodically thawed by war, insurgency, or failed dialogue.

The effects of the war multiplied over the years, shaping everything from foreign policy to internal security. The region became heavily militarised, and generations of Kashmiris were raised amid checkpoints, curfews, and the constant presence of armed forces. The wounds of Partition deepened in Kashmir, where fear and uncertainty became part of everyday life. The war's legacy was not confined to the LoC; it spread into the corridors of diplomacy, where every bilateral meeting, every summit, every UN General Assembly reference carried the burden of this unresolved chapter.

Yet, while the gunfire may have ceased in 1949, the war never truly ended. It transformed. It became an insurgency, a battleground for proxy warfare, a canvas for global players to project their interests. The echoes of that first war can be heard in the silence after a blast, in the slogans on city walls, in the guarded optimism of peace talks, and in the cautious speeches made in international forums.

In August 2019, India altered the trajectory of the issue with one of the most significant constitutional decisions in its post-independence history: the abrogation of Article 370. This article, which had granted Jammu and Kashmir special status, was seen by the Indian government as an outdated barrier to integration and progress. With it removed, the state was reorganised into two union territories—Jammu and Kashmir and Ladakh. This was not just a legal move, but a deeply political one, reflecting a new chapter in India's vision for the region.

The international response was muted. Pakistan protested loudly, suspended trade and diplomatic ties, and tried to raise the issue in global forums. But the world, grappling with its crises, offered limited engagement. Most nations, either due to strategic interests or respect for India's sovereignty, termed the matter as an internal issue.

On the ground, the situation remains layered and sensitive. While there has been a focus on development, investment, and restoring normalcy, security concerns continue. The scars of decades of unrest are not easily erased. The voices for peace are often drowned out by the memories of violence and the geopolitics of division. Yet amidst this complexity, the people of Kashmir continue to dream of dignity, stability, and a life beyond conflict.

For India, Kashmir today is not just a matter of territorial integrity; it is a question of justice, governance, and national unity. Its diplomacy, especially toward Pakistan, is shaped by a singular and uncompromising principle: peace cannot coexist with terror. Until the infrastructure of terrorism is dismantled, meaningful dialogue will remain elusive.

The 1947-48 war was not simply the first war India fought—it was the opening chapter of its most enduring diplomatic challenge. It revealed the fragility of peace, the limitations of global intervention, and the need for regional solutions rooted in realism and respect. Decades later, the war still speaks—not through the roar of guns, but through diplomatic silence, contested maps, and the quiet resilience of a people caught between history and hope.

Historical Blunders

In the aftermath of independence, India emerged not only as a newly sovereign state but as a civilisation reborn with ideals rooted in democracy, peace, and international cooperation. Nowhere were these ideals more sincerely applied—and more severely tested—than in the case of Jammu and Kashmir. The accession of the princely state to India in 1947 was legal, voluntary, and based on the Instrument of Accession signed by Maharaja Hari Singh. The Indian government, under the leadership of Jawaharlal Nehru, responded swiftly to Pakistan's orchestrated invasion, repelling the tribal militias and stabilising the region. Yet, it was in the decisions that followed—motivated by principle rather than political opportunism—that India, despite its best intentions, made some historical missteps.

One of the most debated actions was India's decision to take the Kashmir issue to the United Nations in January 1948. At a time when military operations were turning in India's favour, and the territory could have been fully reclaimed through armed intervention, the leadership chose to internationalise the matter by appealing to the newly formed global body. This move was not born out of weakness but out of a deep conviction in moral diplomacy and international law. Nehru, a statesman shaped by visions of peaceful coexistence and global solidarity, believed that the United Nations would uphold India's rightful claim and condemn Pakistan's aggression. Yet, in doing so, India inadvertently allowed the issue to shift from a domestic matter of accession to a globalised dispute. While the hope was to garner international support and settle the conflict swiftly, what followed was decades of external interference, ambiguity, and a narrative that framed Kashmir not as part of India's democratic family, but as a disputed territory.

The ceasefire that followed in 1949 is another moment often viewed through the lens of "what could have been." Indian forces had successfully regained significant ground, and military leaders believed a few more weeks of operations could result in complete control of the region. Still, the Indian government, acting under immense humanitarian concern and international persuasion, agreed to halt its advance. That ceasefire, a gesture of restraint and peace, resulted in the establishment of the Line of Control, effectively dividing the state and leaving a substantial portion under Pakistan's control. It was a decision that reflected India's trust in international goodwill, but one that also created a long-term strategic vulnerability. The hope was to resolve the matter through dialogue and legality, but the adversary continued to exploit that division through proxy war and misinformation.

Domestically, India's approach to Kashmir was shaped by a delicate balance between constitutional inclusion and regional autonomy. Article 370, crafted to honour the unique circumstances of accession, was intended as a temporary provision to safeguard local identity while enabling gradual integration. Far from being a concession, it was a promise—a demonstration that India would respect diversity, protect special status, and not impose uniformity on a region recovering from conflict. However, over the decades, the complexity of Article 370 created political confusion, and the Centre's occasional overreach in dismissing state governments or interfering with local processes bred mistrust. These actions were not made in bad faith but were often the result of trying to maintain national unity in the face of separatist threats and growing militancy. Nonetheless, the consequences were stark: a growing emotional distance between Srinagar and New Delhi, and a narrative of alienation that was skillfully exploited by hostile powers.

India's interaction with the Kashmiri people was also affected by the conditions of war and terrorism. While enormous efforts were made to develop the region, build institutions, and support civil society, the relentless infiltration from across the border, the rise of insurgency in the 1990s, and the targeted violence against Kashmiri Pandits created an insecure environment where development often had to wait. In such an environment, it was difficult for the democratic fabric to fully blossom. The Indian state was frequently forced to respond with force to restore law and order, and this created a perception of alienation, particularly among the youth. It is important to remember that even in these conditions, India continued to conduct elections, support education, and invest in the region's future, often under great personal risk to its civil servants and soldiers.

On the diplomatic front, India's steadfast position—that **Kashmir is an integral part of its territory**—remained consistent and legally unshakable. However, in the early decades, India often relied on **moral clarity alone** rather than assertive diplomatic engagement to counter Pakistan's global campaign. While Pakistan used every international platform to project its version of the conflict, India trusted that the truth would prevail on its own merits. That **dignified silence**, though admirable, may have allowed falsehoods to take deeper root in global opinion than they might have otherwise. Only in recent years has India taken a more **proactive approach in reshaping the global narrative**, reminding the world that Kashmir is not a question of secession, but of territorial integrity, constitutional unity, and the rights of all its citizens.

None of these choices was made lightly. They were decisions born in the early morning of independence, when the wounds of partition were fresh, and the future of the republic hung delicately in balance. India chose peace when it could have chosen war. It chose law when it could have relied on power. And it chose dialogue when the world might have accepted domination. In hindsight, some of those choices may have had unintended consequences. But in the arc of history, they reflect a nation that always aspired to be better, to act responsibly, and to treat even its most sensitive regions with fairness and hope.

India has learned from the past, refined its policies, and continues to seek a future where Kashmir is not just a part of its map but an inseparable part of its heart. Recognising the missteps does not mean diminishing India's cause—it means strengthening it with truth, humility, and the wisdom to chart a better path forward.

CHAPTER 2

Tricolour Talks: Global Crises

Bharat as Vishwa Guru

The idea of *Vishwa Guru*—a teacher to the world—is not just a flattering phrase tossed around in speeches or headlines. It is a sacred identity born from thousands of years of civilisational wisdom, of values passed not by conquest but by conscience. To be a Vishwa Guru is not to claim superiority; it is to carry responsibility. Bharat has long worn this responsibility like a second skin, not as a nation chasing power, but as a civilisation guided by purpose. And it is in times of global crisis—when the world trembles in uncertainty—that this ancient soul of India rises most visibly, offering light not just to itself but to all corners of the Earth.

To understand why Bharat holds the position of a Vishwa Guru, one must first understand what makes such a title meaningful. A Vishwa Guru is not measured by GDP or nuclear arsenals—it is measured by how it reacts when humanity is on its knees. When borders are shut, when hands are clenched in fear, when voices go silent under war, famine, or disease—a Vishwa Guru speaks not of its own suffering but rushes to ease that of others. Bharat has never tried to dominate through aggression or influence through manipulation. Instead, it has chosen the longer, harder path of leading by example. Its wisdom flows not from strategy rooms but from scriptures, not from cold diplomacy but from warm human values.

This identity did not begin in the modern era—it began in antiquity. From the days of **Nalanda** and **Takshashila**, where knowledge from around the world gathered like rivers to an ocean, to the message of **Buddha** that travelled across Asia bearing the gift of peace, Bharat has always given without asking. Even empires that ruled its lands could not conquer their spirit. And as time moved forward, so did Bharat's mission—to not just preserve its own civilisation, but to uplift the global one. This spiritual legacy continued through the teachings of **Swami Vivekananda**, whose message of unity and tolerance echoed across continents. But it wasn't just words—it became policy, action, and character.

But Bharat's role as a global caregiver didn't stop with its early years. In recent decades, its spirit of humanity has only grown stronger. As the world faced the biggest health crisis in a century—COVID-19—many nations turned inward. Supplies were hoarded. Borders were sealed. But Bharat looked outward. Even as its own population suffered, it launched one of the largest humanitarian missions the world had seen: ***Vaccine Maitri***. Millions of vaccine doses were sent to over a hundred countries—some wealthier than India, some barely known. It didn't matter. What mattered was the life behind every request. Bharat knew that true recovery meant no one could be left behind.

Even in moments of economic collapse, as seen in Sri Lanka, Bharat didn't play the predator. It extended lines of credit, sent fuel, food, and medicine, not with conditions, but with care. It didn't exploit its neighbour's weakness—it protected their dignity. In Africa, India continues to build—not empires, but ecosystems. Schools, hospitals, solar parks—all standing as quiet markers of a country that believes help must be given before it is asked. In global platforms, from the UN to the G20, India has become the voice for those often unheard—the Global South, the forgotten middle. In its G20 presidency, it didn't just represent itself—it represented every smaller nation that never gets a seat at the big table. With the theme *One Earth, One Family, One Future*, Bharat reminded the world that development cannot be selfish, and progress must include the last, the lost, and the least.

Bharat's strength lies in this consistency. Whether under Nehru or Modi, the principle has remained the same—serve the world without expecting applause. It is a country that responds not just with arms and ammunition, but with ambulances and affection. It is a nation that knows the power of words but chooses the nobility of deeds. While many countries flex their muscles, Bharat extends its hands. In times of disaster, disease, or displacement, India doesn't ask "what's in it for me?" It asks, "What can I give?"

To be a Vishwa Guru, one must not rise above the world, but stand within it, and still choose kindness. Bharat has done that, again and again. Not by shouting on rooftops, but by showing up at the doorsteps of despair. That is not just foreign policy. That is a moral compass. That is not just a strategy. That is the soul.

In times of crisis, when the world has stumbled, Bharat has not walked ahead—it has turned around, extended a hand, and said, "Let's go together."

And that is why, even when maps change and powers rise and fall, Bharat's place remains unshaken—not just in history, but in the heart of humanity.

From the earliest scriptures to the modern international stage, India has been guided by the principle of ***Vasudhaiva Kutumbakam***—the world is one family. This core belief has shaped its diplomatic identity for centuries. In times of global upheaval, Bharat has consistently shown that leadership is not always about being the most powerful—it is about being the most present, the most prepared, and the most peaceful.

India's legacy as a global thought leader begins with its ancient philosophical traditions, but it has also evolved through its modern history. During the mid-20th century, in the aftermath of its hard-won independence, Bharat under the visionary leadership of Prime Minister **Jawaharlal Nehru**, became a moral voice in a divided world. The Cold War was intensifying, alliances were hardening, and ideological blocs were forming—but India chose a different path: **non-alignment**.

Nehru's diplomacy emphasised sovereignty, peace, and dialogue. The **Non-Aligned Movement**, co-founded by India, gave newly liberated nations a platform to assert their identities without aligning with any power bloc. India's role in shaping this space was not merely political—it was deeply humanitarian. It gave a voice to the voiceless and dignity to those just beginning their journey as free nations.

India also became one of the largest contributors to **United Nations peacekeeping operations**. Indian forces have served in some of the most challenging missions, bringing stability to conflict zones in Africa, Asia, and the Middle East. These deployments were never acts of interference but of protection, offered with humility and rooted in duty.

As the world entered the 21st century, the nature of global crises changed—pandemics, climate emergencies, conflicts, and humanitarian breakdowns began to test international solidarity. In each of these moments, Bharat reaffirmed its timeless values through modern action.

This was not an isolated act. In times of war and conflict, India prioritised rescue and relief. ***Operation Ganga,*** during the war in Ukraine, successfully evacuated thousands of Indian students stranded in the region, often amid crossfire and chaos. Beyond its citizens, India also extended evacuation support to nationals of neighbouring countries—a gesture of shared humanity.

Similarly, ***Operation Devi Shakti*** in Afghanistan brought Indian citizens and Afghan partners safely home after the Taliban takeover. ***Operation Kaveri*** in Sudan and ***Operation Rahat*** in Yemen reflected India's consistent ability to act swiftly and compassionately, guided by responsibility rather than rhetoric. India's humanitarian engagements extend far beyond rescue. From delivering food and fuel to Sri Lanka during its economic crisis, to providing disaster relief to Nepal after its devastating earthquakes, and sending aid to Turkey during its recent earthquakes, India's hand of friendship has always reached far, yet remained grounded in humility. These acts are not announcements of power—they are affirmations of purpose. India does not seek applause or reward. Its diplomacy is often quiet, but always steady. Whether it is building hospitals in Africa, training peacekeepers, providing digital education to remote corners of the world, or offering development assistance in Southeast Asia and the Indian Ocean region, India's global footprint is marked by empathy, not ego.

The Continuity of Vision: From Nehru to Modi

From Nehru's moral diplomacy, through Atal Bihari Vajpayee's emphasis on "India's place in the comity of nations," and Dr. Manmohan Singh's economic diplomacy, and now Prime Minister Narendra Modi's articulation of *One Earth, One Family, One Future*—India's foreign policy has carried forward a consistent thread of global responsibility.

Today, India's leadership in forums like the G20, BRICS, and the UN showcases its belief in inclusive growth and global cooperation. Initiatives like the International Solar Alliance and the Coalition for Disaster Resilient Infrastructure further exemplify India's forward-looking diplomacy, rooted in sustainability, equity, and collective well-being.

India's diplomatic journey has never been static — it has pulsed with the rhythm of shifting global winds, internal transformations, and the personal philosophies of each leader. From Nehru's idealistic dawn to Modi's assertive twilight diplomacy, the arc of Indian foreign policy has travelled across a dramatic spectrum — sometimes with grace, sometimes with grit, and sometimes with grey undertones that history continues to debate.

Pandit Jawaharlal Nehru, India's first Prime Minister, wasn't just building dams and drafting five-year plans — he was also building India's identity on the world stage. Rooted in principles of non-violence and moral leadership, his diplomacy rejected the Cold War's binary and chose the middle path: the Non-Aligned Movement (NAM). He wanted India to be a voice for the decolonised, the oppressed, and the ignored. Under his leadership, India spoke boldly against apartheid, colonialism, and war, emerging as the conscience-keeper of the Third World. His vision was lofty — he dreamt of India not just as a nation, but as a moral compass for humanity.

And yet, the very moralism that defined Nehru also shackled him. He trusted China, famously spoke of *"Hindi-Chini Bhai Bhai,"* and hesitated to militarise borders — a gamble that cost India dearly in the 1962 war. His refusal to align militarily, even strategically, made India vulnerable. Was moral high ground enough in a world ruled by missiles, alliances, and espionage? Could a newly independent nation afford such romanticism?

Then came Indira Gandhi — and with her, a storm. If Nehru was diplomacy with a dove, Indira was diplomacy with a dagger wrapped in silk. Her leadership during the 1971 Bangladesh Liberation War showed India shedding its softness. She signed a treaty with the Soviet Union, defied American pressure, and decisively split Pakistan in two — a masterstroke of realpolitik. Under her, India tested its first nuclear weapon in 1974, signalling to the world that India could not be bullied. And yet, the Emergency of 1975 and her centralisation of power domestically raised a haunting question: can strong foreign policy forgive democratic erosion at home?

Rajiv Gandhi brought in a breeze of modernity — young, tech-savvy, and globally attuned. He initiated new friendships with the US and East Asia, and dared to send Indian troops to Sri Lanka in a controversial peacekeeping mission. While visionary in tech diplomacy, he proved less seasoned in military foresight, and India subsequently paid the price when the IPKF mission turned violent. His assassination itself was a grim lesson in the unintended consequences of foreign interventions.

The post-liberalisation era of the 1990s brought a new wave of diplomatic shifts. P.V. Narasimha Rao, often under-credited, quietly shifted India from non-alignment to multi-alignment. He opened full diplomatic ties with Israel, started 'Look East Policy', and stabilised relations with the West. Atal Bihari Vajpayee took it forward with boldness — India conducted nuclear tests in 1998 despite international pressure and yet managed to open dialogue with the US and even Pakistan. His Lahore bus diplomacy was a symbol of courage; the Kargil War that followed tested that courage. Still, Vajpayee showed statesmanship by not allowing military success to derail diplomatic sanity.

Then came Dr. Manmohan Singh — quiet but calculated. Under his leadership, India signed the historic Indo-US Nuclear Deal, breaking decades of nuclear apartheid. His economic diplomacy elevated India's image as a responsible global power. Yet, critics questioned whether his foreign policy was too passive, and whether his silence allowed China to grow aggressive along our borders and in multilateral spaces.

Now, with Prime Minister Narendra Modi, Indian diplomacy has become louder, more visible, and unapologetically assertive. His visits abroad are often theatrical, but not hollow — they've brought real gains. India's Vaccine Maitri initiative during COVID-19 transformed it into the **pharmacy of the world**. Rescue missions like **Operation Ganga** and **Vande Bharat** showcased India as a guardian for its diaspora. The 'Act East Policy' got teeth, relations with Gulf nations bloomed, and QUAD revived under his watch. India stood its ground at Galwan and walked out of RCEP, showing it's no longer shy of confrontation. From popularising yoga at the UN to G20 presidency, Modi has positioned India as a 'Vishwa Guru' in global discourse.

But this transformation hasn't come without shadows. Critics argue that soft power is being replaced with chest-thumping, that strategic autonomy is increasingly leaning towards Western camps, and that domestic polarisation could be affecting India's global perception. The balancing act between self-interest and moral responsibility is currently being tested—much like Nehru's era, but with different stakes.

So where do we stand? From Nehru's dream of peaceful leadership to Modi's drive for global prominence, India's diplomacy profoundly reflects its evolving soul. Neither extreme is perfect. Both idealism and realism have shown their limits. But together, they tell the story of a nation still learning how to lead—not just with power, but with purpose. The question remains: will India be remembered as a moral power, a strategic power, or a rare fusion of both?

Beyond the Spotlight: Unveiling India's Diplomatic Blind Spots

India's foreign policy, from the era of Nehru to Modi, reads like a complex saga—one filled with towering ideals, strategic gambits, and a fair share of missteps wrapped in layers of silence. It is a story often narrated in celebratory tones or glossed over with patriotic fervor, but the real test of a nation's diplomacy lies in its ability to face its own contradictions with courage, humility, and pride. So, let's embark on an honest exploration – not to undermine the legacy but to enrich it with questions few dare to ask.

Jawaharlal Nehru, the visionary who sculpted India's initial diplomatic contours, is revered for his idealism and moral clarity. The Non-Aligned Movement (NAM), under his stewardship, projected India as the conscience of the post-colonial world, refusing to bow before the binary Cold War pressures. However, therein lies a paradox worth pondering. Nehru's steadfast faith in the United Nations, a body often held hostage by the veto powers, arguably delayed India's readiness for the harsh realities of geopolitical power play. The Kashmir dispute was repeatedly taken to the UN with hopes of peaceful resolution, but the institution's inability to act decisively—seen in failures across Korea, Palestine, and Hungary—was a glaring red flag ignored. Was this unwavering faith an act of profound idealism or perhaps diplomatic naivety? While standing tall on principles is noble, was India inadvertently shackling itself by anchoring hope in a faltering international system? The lesson is clear: ideals must be balanced with pragmatic foresight; a nation cannot wage war on hope alone.

Indira Gandhi's tenure brought a dramatic shift—a blend of steely resolve and pragmatic aggression. Her orchestration of the 1971 Bangladesh Liberation War was undeniably a masterstroke, elevating India's stature and rewriting South Asia's map. Yet, the diplomatic aftermath invites critical reflection. The Simla Agreement, often celebrated as the peace accord of its time, left critical strategic opportunities unseized. The early release of 90,000 Pakistani Prisoners of War (POWs) and the absence of an explicit, immediate recognition of Bangladesh by Pakistan arguably left India vulnerable to future tensions. Did exhaustion or a desire for quick peace cause India to accept a fragile agreement? Or was it a missed chance to cement a lasting regional order decisively in India's favor? Diplomatic victories, after all, are measured not just by the battlefield gains, but by the strength and durability of peace treaties.

Narasimha Rao's era introduced economic liberalization and a recalibration of foreign relations, including the bold outreach to Israel. However, India's silence during the Oslo Accords—an unprecedented peace initiative between Israel and

Palestine—raises intriguing questions. Given India's historical support for Palestine and emerging ties with Israel, this could have been a golden moment for New Delhi to act as a unique bridge in a conflict that has long baffled the world. Was India's silence a cautious strategic choice, or a missed opportunity to assert itself as a global peacemaker in the Middle East? Playing the sidelines might be safe, but sometimes renders a nation invisible.

Atal Bihari Vajpayee's period was marked by an assertive nuclear policy coupled with daring diplomatic overtures. His government's nuclear tests in 1998 broke decades of restraint and sent a clear message: India had arrived. Yet, the Kargil conflict severely tested the durability of his dual approach. India's measured restraint—refraining from crossing the Line of Control—was hailed internationally, but it also raises a strategic dilemma. Could a more aggressive response, remaining within the limits of international law, have compelled Pakistan to fundamentally rethink its proxy war strategies? India's restraint was a moral high ground, but did it also leave the door open for future provocations? Diplomacy is a delicate dance between strength and subtlety, and sometimes the rhythm indeed can be misread.

Dr. Manmohan Singh's tenure brought a veneer of calm professionalism to foreign policy, epitomized by the landmark Indo-US Nuclear Deal. This repositioned India in the global nuclear order, gaining both respect and strategic partnership. Nonetheless, during this period, China's steady encroachment along the Himalayan borders went largely unchallenged in international forum. Why did India's diplomacy hesitate to robustly confront China's salami-slicing tactics in platforms such as BRICS or the SCO, where China sought to cement its leadership? Quiet diplomacy has its merits, but when silence becomes acquiescence, it risks emboldening adversaries.

Narendra Modi's diplomatic style is unmistakably assertive and highly visible. His government's proactive outreach—spanning from Africa to the Gulf, from vaccine diplomacy during the COVID-19 pandemic to championing initiatives like QUAD—signals a confident India stepping onto the world stage. However, the grandeur of global summits and spectacular rallies like 'Howdy Modi' or 'Namaste Trump' must be examined critically. Beyond optics, what concrete diplomatic gains have these events delivered? Moreover, India's continued underinvestment in its diplomatic corps is a puzzle. How does a country aspiring to be a global leader manage with one of the lowest ratios of foreign service officers per capita among major economies? Is this a strategic oversight or a reflection of misplaced priorities?

India's withdrawal from multilateral deals like the Regional Comprehensive Economic Partnership (RCEP), while framed as protecting domestic interests, also suggests a reluctance to fully embrace the complexities of economic globalization fully. Could a more nuanced, patient approach have allowed India to better integrate into Asia's fast-evolving trade landscape without compromising its core interests? Nationalistic pride is vital, but so is strategic patience and adaptability.

On the environmental front, India's moral stance on climate justice resonates globally, especially as the definitive voice of the Global South. Yet, the country has yet to fully harness its full diplomatic potential to lead a coalition that proactively shapes the global climate agenda rather than merely responding to it. The world looks to India not only to join summits but to actively write the script of climate equity and green innovation.

At the heart of every diplomatic decision lies a profound choice—not merely about power or prestige, but about **humanity over hatred**. This chapter's exploration of India's foreign policy journey is far more than a critique of strategies and treaties; fundamentally it is a call to place human values at the core of international relations. When Nehru pushed for peace and non-alignment, or when Indira Gandhi led a decisive war to end immense suffering in East Pakistan, these were not mere political maneuvers—they were earnest attempts to prioritize the dignity and lives of millions over cycles of violence and suspicion. However, diplomacy that misses key opportunities, tolerates ambiguity, or opts for silence in the face of injustice risks perpetuating the very hatred it seeks to overcome.

Understanding the **nuances, the successes, and the failures** in India's diplomatic history helps us see the vital link between statecraft and humanitarian ideals. If diplomacy becomes an exercise solely in realpolitik, it loses the power to transform conflict into coexistence, rivalry into respect. By rigorously questioning India's choices, this chapter encourages a broader vision—one where national interest and global justice are not enemies but partners in creating a world where **hatred yields to humanity**. This is not just about India's past or future on the global stage; it is about shaping a legacy where diplomacy serves as an enduring bridge to peace, dignity, and shared human progress.

"In a world where lines on maps often define enemies, the true challenge of diplomacy is to redraw those lines in hearts. Humanity over hatred isn't just a slogan; it is the bedrock of lasting peace. When nations choose empathy over enmity, dialogue over destruction, they unlock the true potential of diplomacy—not as a game of power, but as a sacred

responsibility to protect life, dignity, and hope. India's unique philosophical heritage and its modern diplomatic efforts show us that the future belongs to those who dare to put humanity first, even when hatred seeks to drag us backward."

"Challenges on the Road to Vishwa Guru"

But no vision of greatness is complete without reflection. To truly wear the mantle of a *Vishwa Guru*, Bharat must also confront the mirror, not to diminish itself, but to refine its path. Because the journey of being a guiding light to the world must begin with lighting every corner of one's own home.

India's humanitarian diplomacy is noble and inspiring, but it coexists with contradictions that demand acknowledgement. One of the most pressing concerns is the gap between ***external generosity* and *internal adequacy***. While the world applauds India's role in dispatching vaccines, oxygen, and food aid to dozens of countries, many Indian citizens, especially in rural belts, still face inadequate access to basic healthcare, education, clean drinking water, and sanitation. The stark divide between India's global outreach and local outreach is a shadow that risks dimming its moral light.

The second challenge lies in **bureaucratic inertia** and **execution delays**. India is abundant in vision but often stumbles in implementation. Many foreign policy initiatives lack follow-through or become entangled in red tape, losing momentum after the headlines fade. Whether it is the disbursal of aid, evacuation operations, or diplomatic promises to smaller nations—what begins with thunder sometimes ends in whispers. For Bharat to be trusted as a long-term pillar of hope, *consistency* must match *compassion*.

Then comes the question of **global perception versus geopolitical silence**. India's deliberate neutrality on certain humanitarian crises, like its cautious stance on the Rohingya crisis, or hesitations to take sides during ongoing wars, has drawn global criticism. While it follows a doctrine of strategic autonomy and non-interference, the absence of vocal solidarity in some international humanitarian causes makes it vulnerable to accusations of moral ambiguity. If India aspires to be the world's conscience, it must also risk speaking uncomfortable truths—not just in private chambers but in global forums.

Furthermore, there's an **economic constraint**. India's resources, though vast, are not limitless. Balancing domestic welfare with international aid is a tightrope act. At times, the public questions the logic behind large aid packages when local infrastructure still gasps for funding. To overcome this, India must expand its fiscal space through sustainable economic reforms, reduce dependency on imports in key sectors, and build a model of "development diplomacy" where global help leads to mutual economic growth, not one-sided expenditure.

And then, there's the **need for an inclusive narrative**. India's humanitarian missions are sometimes viewed as top-down gestures rather than people-driven movements. If Bharat wishes to present itself as a beacon of *collective human care,* it must better involve its youth, civil society, and private sector in diplomacy. Universities should teach global ethics. Schools should raise global citizens. NGOs and entrepreneurs should be empowered to represent India's goodwill abroad, not just diplomats and ministers.

Yet, none of these are permanent flaws—they are fixable, evolving, and within reach. And Bharat, perhaps more than any other country, has the *moral courage* to self-correct. To bridge the gap between promise and practice, India must create synergy between domestic upliftment and global outreach. It must embrace "*Jan Bhagidari*" – people's participation — in foreign policy. It must digitise aid flows, ensuring public accountability for humanitarian missions, and build global volunteer programs that let every Indian become an unofficial ambassador of compassion.

What makes Bharat special is not that it never falters — it's that it consistently learns, adapts, and rises again with deeper wisdom. These challenges are not the end of its Vishwa Guru dream — they are the very fire that will forge it. If India faces them head-on, with transparency, innovation, and inclusion, its leadership will not just be admired — it will be trusted.

In the end, greatness is not born from pretending to be flawless. It is born from the strength to admit what must be improved and the will to improve it.

And that — more than any slogan or summit — is the true sign of a ***Vishwa Guru in the making for India that is more Bharat.***

The Tiranga: A Beacon of Hope and Humanity in Times of Crisis

In moments of global crisis, when the world stands at the brink of despair, there rises a symbol — a symbol that transcends borders, a symbol that offers not just hope, but a profound sense of purpose and unity. This is India's Tiranga, the Tricolour, a flag that stands as a living testament to a nation that believes in peace, compassion, and unwavering support for all. The Tiranga — with its vibrant saffron, white, and green stripes — represents far more than just a country's identity. It represents the hope of the world, the unbroken spirit of humanity, and the power of solidarity.

When nations are struck by disaster, war, or pandemic, it is the Tiranga that consistently rises above all, reminding the world of India's steadfast commitment to peace, cooperation, and humanitarian aid. The saffron stripe, which symbolises courage, speaks volumes about India's willingness to go beyond its borders, to stretch out a hand to those in need, no matter the cost. This is the same courage that led India to stand tall during Operation Ganga, bringing back its citizens from the war-torn areas of Ukraine, showing the world that when crisis strikes, India will not hesitate to act, will not hesitate to save lives, to protect its people, and to extend its care to the helpless. The saffron is more than just a colour—it's the very heartbeat of a nation that chooses to fight for others, to offer a lifeline when the world seems lost.

And then there is the white stripe in the Tiranga, the colour that represents peace. It is a message not only to India's people but to the world—that peace is always the answer. In times when bombs fall and hatred spreads like wildfire, India chooses diplomacy. India chooses dialogue. India chooses the soft power of influence over the roar of war. The white of the Tiranga tells the world that while others may choose to burn bridges, India will always build them. Whether it's offering humanitarian aid, sending peacekeepers, or contributing to peace processes, India's voice on the global stage is one of peace and non-violence, echoing the timeless teachings of Mahatma Gandhi and the path of diplomacy. In times of a global pandemic, India embraced the call of humanity, producing and distributing vaccines for all, even when many were hoarding resources. This was India's commitment to the world—that humanity comes first.

The green stripe of the Tiranga, representing prosperity and harmony, speaks volumes about India's mission to help the world rise together. It stands for the understanding that true progress cannot exist in a world where some thrive while others suffer. India's philosophy has always been to work for the collective good, striving for a future where no nation is left behind. The green is not just a colour; it is a promise. It is the promise of aid when nations are struck by calamity, whether it be the aftermath of natural disasters in Nepal, Sri Lanka, or Bangladesh, or offering crucial medical assistance during global health emergencies. It is the colour of compassion, of doing what's right, of standing together in the face of adversity.

In every crisis, be it global pandemics, armed conflicts, or humanitarian disasters, the Tiranga symbolises not just India's actions but its very soul. When the world looks at India, it sees a nation that is always ready to act, always ready to stand with those in need. In **Operation Rahat**, India's swift response to the Nepal earthquake, to its its ongoing relief efforts for refugees, India's Tiranga has indeed become a symbol of hope. The nation's commitment to humanitarian aid is not just a matter of policy, it's a profound reflection of its DNA—a nation that deeply understands the value of life, and the immense power of coming together, especially in the darkest moments.

The Tiranga, therefore, represents a vision—a vision of a better world where borders do not divide us, where humanity truly comes first, and where a nation's strength lies not just in its military might but in its unwavering ability to uplift others. It tells the world that India's foreign policy will always centre around peace, humanity, and the collective welfare of all nations. When global crises arise, the Tiranga reminds the world that India will not just stand by and watch. It will rise, not with the fury of war, but with the strength of compassion, the force of diplomacy, and the resolute will to make the world a better place for all.

As India continues to stand tall in the global arena, the Tiranga will forever wave, reminding every citizen of the world that India is with you, not just as a nation but as a partner, a helper, and a leader in humanitarian causes. In times of crisis, when all seems lost, India's Tiranga will be the light that shows the way, because it is not just a symbol of India—it is a symbol of hope for the world.

"In India's gentle embrace, the world feels love again, rediscovers its soul—where humanity triumphs over hatred"

Trump and Elon Musk: from Collabaration to Confrontation

When Donald Trump launched his presidential campaign in 2015, Elon Musk largely stayed away from partisan endorsements. As the CEO of Tesla and SpaceX, Musk remained focused on innovation and environmental sustainability—values that often contrasted with Trump's policies. During Trump's first term (2017–2021), Musk served briefly on two White House business advisory councils. However, he **publicly resigned from both in 2017**, following Trump's decision to withdraw from the **Paris Climate Agreement**. Musk stated, "Climate change is real. Leaving Paris is not good for America or the world." This marked the first visible fracture between the two men, as Musk chose principle over proximity to power.

Despite these differences, Musk and Trump occasionally found common ground—particularly around space exploration and deregulation. Under Trump, NASA's Artemis program accelerated, benefiting SpaceX contracts. Meanwhile, Trump praised Musk as "one of our great geniuses" during a 2020 rally, signaling mutual, if cautious, respect. Still, Musk kept a distance from openly endorsing Trump, choosing instead to advocate for technological advancement and innovation in a politically neutral tone.

The period following the 2020 election—which Trump falsely claimed was "stolen"—saw Musk grow increasingly disenchanted with mainstream political and media narratives. While not a Trump supporter during the 2020 campaign, Musk became sharply critical of **censorship, lockdowns, and government overreach**, particularly on platforms like Twitter.

By 2022, Musk's focus shifted heavily toward **free speech advocacy**. His **acquisition of Twitter (renamed X)** was framed as a crusade against what he saw as "woke tyranny" and liberal groupthink. This is where Musk's worldview began aligning more closely with Trump's populist base, though not necessarily with Trump himself. Notably, after Musk took over Twitter, he reinstated Trump's suspended account following the January 6 Capitol riot—but **Trump declined to return**, remaining on his own platform, Truth Social.

Still, the ideological alignment deepened. Musk began criticizing the Biden administration over electric vehicle subsidies that excluded Tesla, and lamented the influence of unelected bureaucracies. His political commentary became more conservative, positioning him as a powerful voice among anti-establishment, libertarian-leaning circles. Though not yet formal allies, Musk and Trump were increasingly swimming in the same pool of political influence.

Everything changed on **July 13, 2024**, when Trump survived an **assassination attempt** during a rally in Butler, Pennsylvania. The attempt—widely broadcast and deeply polarizing—sparked national outrage and renewed Trump's political momentum. Musk, who had previously been reluctant to fully endorse any candidate, emerged as one of Trump's **most vocal backers** in the wake of the attack.

Musk declared on X that America was at a "turning point" and that Trump's survival was a sign of destiny. Over the next three months, Musk **personally donated over $277 million** to pro-Trump super PACs, becoming the **largest individual donor of the 2024 election cycle**. His social-media platform, X, functioned as a digital campaign machine, amplifying Trump's messaging, attacking opponents, and mobilizing conservative youth. Musk also appeared **at campaign rallies wearing MAGA caps**, sharing stages with Trump and conducting live-streamed interviews that reached tens of millions of viewers.

This culminated on **Inauguration Day 2025**, when Trump—returning to office—**appointed Musk as a "Special Government Employee"** tasked with co-leading the newly created **Department of Government Efficiency (DOGE)**. The goal was to streamline bureaucracy, cut waste, and digitize federal systems. It marked an unprecedented fusion of Silicon Valley and Washington, with Musk symbolizing a new elite class that blurred the line between private innovation and public governance.

But the honeymoon did not last.

By March 2025, deep fissures emerged between Musk and Trump over fiscal policy. Trump introduced the **"One Big Beautiful Bill,"** a massive legislative package that slashed taxes while increasing defense and infrastructure spending. The Congressional Budget Office warned that it would **add over $2.3 trillion to the national debt** over the next decade. Musk, a self-proclaimed "fiscal realist," **denounced the bill publicly**, accusing Trump of "destroying the dollar" and failing to rein in bureaucratic corruption.

Tensions boiled over when Musk **suggested impeachment** if Trump refused to declassify files related to **Jeffrey Epstein**, which Musk believed implicated elites across political lines. Trump retaliated viciously, calling Musk "ungrateful," "disloyal," and accusing him of "siding with the Deep State." Trump even threatened to **revoke SpaceX and Tesla's federal contracts**—a move that shook markets.

The backlash was immediate. **Tesla's share price dropped over 14%**, wiping out more than **$150 billion in market value** in a week. SpaceX faced review of NASA and Pentagon contracts, with aerospace insiders warning of a "politically motivated purge." Musk responded defiantly on X, stating that "liberty cannot exist without transparency," and accusing the Trump administration of betraying its promise to disrupt the status quo.

Meanwhile, Trump forged ahead with a radically nationalist second-term agenda. In **February 2025**, his administration imposed **25% tariffs** on goods from Canada and Mexico and **10% on Chinese imports**, upending more than **$2 trillion in annual trade**. Economists warned of inflation and retaliatory trade wars. American automakers, many of which relied on cross-border supply chains, braced for job losses and production cuts.

In **June 2025**, Trump issued a sweeping **executive order banning citizens of twelve Muslim and African countries**, expanding on his earlier travel bans. The African Union condemned the move as "racist and colonial," and lawsuits flooded federal courts.

Even more controversially, Trump **revoked Harvard University's right to enroll new international students**, citing "national security concerns" and alleged "foreign ideological influence." Over **1.1 million international students** across the U.S. were affected. The Department of Homeland Security began enhanced social-media surveillance of visa applicants linked to Harvard and other elite institutions. A federal judge soon **blocked the order**, calling it unconstitutional, but the damage was done: global trust in the U.S. as an education hub began to erode.

The fallout of the Musk–Trump break and Trump's polarizing agenda sent shockwaves through politics, business, and diplomacy. Most Republican lawmakers sided with Trump, fearing that supporting Musk would split the base. Conservative media labeled Musk a **"traitor to MAGA,"** while liberal outlets viewed him as a **"misguided techno-populist."** Musk, for his part, continued using X to champion free speech, fiscal reform, and transparency—but the political establishment largely distanced itself.

Financial markets became more volatile. Tech stocks slumped, foreign investment slowed, and universities scrambled to protect their international student pipelines. Traditional U.S. allies abroad questioned Washington's commitment to global norms, while authoritarian regimes applauded the chaos as proof that American democracy was self-destructing.

Historians and political analysts have begun to frame this chapter as **a cautionary tale: a collision between populism and technocracy, ego and ideology, private power and public office.** The Musk–Trump saga—once hailed as a revolutionary partnership—now stands as a vivid example of how unstructured alliances, driven more by charisma than coherent policy, can implode spectacularly under the weight of ambition, disagreement, and unchecked executive authority.

In the grand continuum of modern political history, the convergence of Donald Trump's illiberal populism with the authoritarian patterns of Adolf Hitler, while distinct in chronology and execution, signals **an ominous revival of**

autocracy cloaked in the aesthetics of democracy. Hitler's ascent in 1933 was facilitated by a perfect storm of hyperinflation, national humiliation post-Versailles, and mass unemployment, which he weaponized through the rhetoric of racial purity, anti-intellectualism, and a mythical reclamation of national pride—codified in **the Nazi slogan of *Ein Volk, ein Reich, ein Führer***. Donald Trump's 21st-century rise drew from a similar emotional reservoir: economic insecurity among the white working class, a perceived cultural displacement, and a yearning for the restoration of a lost American grandeur. **His rallying cry, "Make America Great Again,"** was not merely a political slogan but a psychological invocation—mirroring Hitler's promise to "restore Germany's greatness"—that offered a singular figure as the savior of a fractured nation.

Both men meticulously crafted a cult of personality, leveraging mass media to engineer loyalty not to the constitution, but to themselves. Hitler had Leni Riefenstahl's propaganda films and the Reich Ministry of Public Enlightenment; Trump harnessed the 24/7 spectacle of Fox News, Twitter (now X), and Truth Social to create an alternate reality, resistant to fact and immune to dissent. Just as Hitler exploited the Reichstag Fire to centralize power under the guise of national security, Trump in his second term has sought to override institutional guardrails via executive orders, defiance of judicial independence, and a dismantling of bureaucratic norms—all under the justification of restoring "law and order."

The parallels intensified in early 2025, when Trump initiated sweeping measures reminiscent of historical ethnic and ideological purges: mass deportations targeting undocumented immigrants, a blanket ban on international students from elite universities under the pretext of national security, and aggressive tariff regimes aimed at asserting economic autarky. These policies, while not genocidal in intent, evoke chilling echoes of the early years of the Third Reich, where legalistic repression laid the groundwork for systemic violence. The façade of legality—border enforcement, trade wars, visa restrictions—masked a deeper philosophical alignment: the belief that a nation's strength lies in its homogeneity, its cultural purity, and its centralization of power in a strongman figure.

The symbolic crescendo of this ideological convergence arrived at a 2025 global tech summit, where Elon Musk—visionary entrepreneur turned techno-authoritarian—was photographed standing beside Trump, raising his right arm in a gesture disturbingly similar to the infamous Nazi salute. Though Musk's representatives hastily dismissed the gesture as an "awkward wave," the historical connotation was unmistakable. The image rapidly went viral, sparking condemnation from Holocaust remembrance institutions, international human rights bodies, and historians of fascism. For many, it wasn't merely a misstep—**it was the crystallization of a new authoritarian axis: one in which state power and technological dominance coalesce under the guise of freedom and innovation.**

Musk, who once symbolized the future of human progress through ventures like SpaceX, Neuralink, and Tesla, had by this point become a central figure in the architecture of global misinformation. His acquisition of Twitter (renamed X) resulted in the reinstatement of deplatformed extremists, the erosion of content moderation, and the normalization of hate speech, conspiracies, and political propaganda. While Hitler required Joseph Goebbels to control the message, Trump and

Musk benefited from **algorithmic echo chambers** and unregulated digital platforms to saturate the public sphere with ideological distortions.

The alliance—however fractured by egos, financial disputes, and political divergence—represented **a dark prototype of 21st-century fascism**. Unlike the overt totalitarianism of the 1930s, this iteration wears the mask of legality, cloaked in constitutional language, entrepreneurial disruption, and meme culture. It does not march in uniforms, but codes in Silicon Valley; it doesn't burn books, but drowns truth in a deluge of digital disinformation. Trump's demonization of the press as the "enemy of the people," his use of paramilitary forces during protests, and his efforts to criminalize dissent echoed the early repressive tactics of the Nazi regime. Meanwhile, Musk's control over satellites, AI infrastructure, and the public square of global discourse gave him unprecedented soft power—one that, when aligned with an autocrat, becomes not a tool of liberation but of ideological enforcement.

This moment in 2025—one of salutes, silence, and symbolism—must be read not in isolation but as a historical cipher. It reminds us that fascism does not always announce itself through jackboots and swastikas. Sometimes, it arrives with billion-dollar valuations, viral hashtags, and polished charisma. Democracies collapse not only through coups, but through complacency, celebrity, and the slow erosion of norms by those who claim to protect them.

Its creates a sense of curiosity in the minds of world leaders That **Is the World Safe In Hands Of Such? Can World really Trust The Policies and Projects of Tech Giant who Normalises the Use Of *Nazi Salute* ? or Its Just Showcase of power …**

The True Meaning of Peace

Peace is often thought of as simply the absence of war—a brief pause in the otherwise tumultuous saga of human conflict. Yet true peace is far richer, deeper, and more transformative than mere silence after violence. It is a dynamic, active force that shapes the course of history, enabling societies to flourish, cultures to blossom, and humanity to progress beyond the destructive cycle of conflict.

Peace demands courage, wisdom, and an unwavering commitment to justice and human dignity. Unlike power wielded through coercion and force, peace embodies strength through empathy, dialogue, and reconciliation. It is not passive; peace is the highest expression of collective human maturity and aspiration. The power of peace is the power to heal, to rebuild, and to unite. It is the fundamental force that enables diplomacy, sustains development, and fosters genuine global cooperation.

In a world still marred by conflicts, divisions, and mistrust, peace stands as the most urgent and noble goal. This chapter explores peace as a powerful agent of change—one that transcends borders, cultures, and ideologies. It delves into the historical roots of peace, examine the essential role it plays in diplomacy, and explores how cultural exchange fuels its spread. Furthermore, itanalyzes case studies where peace triumphed over power, highlighting the mechanisms and leadership behind transformative peace processes. Finally, it considers the emotional and psychological dimensions of peace and lays out the challenges and pathways to securing a peaceful future.

Peace is not a mere intermission between wars; it is the foundation on which civilizations build their greatest achievements. Throughout history, sustained eras of peace have consistently unlocked unparalleled human potential, nurturing profound advances in science, philosophy, art, and governance.

The remarkable **Pax Romana**, a two-century period of relative peace and stability across the Roman Empire, enabled an unprecedented expansion of infrastructure, commerce, and culture. Roads, aqueducts, and law codes created a network that allowed ideas and goods to flow, fostering prosperity. Although enforced by military power, the **Pax Romana's** true strength lay in the very peace it provided—allowing societies to grow beyond survival to thrive.

In ancient India, Emperor Ashoka's transformation after a brutal war led him to champion nonviolence, tolerance, and welfare. His reign exemplified peace as ethical governance, guiding diverse communities toward coexistence and spiritual growth. Ashoka's promotion of Dharma laid early foundations for cultural and religious harmony across Asia.

The Renaissance period witnessed peace as the fertile soil for intellectual and artistic rebirth. After centuries marked by persistent feudal strife, the emergence of relative stability allowed thinkers to question, explore, and innovate—ushering in the Enlightenment and shaping modernity. Peace was not simply the absence of conflict; it was the creative condition enabling humanity's progress.

The 20th century, scarred by two world wars, also saw humanity's most ambitious peace efforts. The League of Nations and later the United Nations embodied the global desire to prevent war through diplomacy, dialogue, and collective security. These institutions made peace a shared international responsibility, transcending national interests.

These historical examples show that peace requires deliberate cultivation and is inseparable from justice, dialogue, and human empathy. It is the prerequisite for sustainable progress, the invisible force underpinning all great human achievement. Diplomacy, in essence, is the practice and art of managing relations between nations through dialogue, negotiation, and mutual understanding rather than through force. It is the language peace speaks in the corridors of power.

Without peace, diplomacy is impossible—talks become threats, negotiations break down, and mistrust escalates. But with peace as the guiding principle, diplomacy transforms conflict into collaboration and hostility into partnership.

International organizations like the United Nations, the European Union, and regional bodies serve as platforms where peace and diplomacy meet. They empower countries to effectively resolve disputes, coordinate policies, and address global challenges collectively.

Effective diplomacy requires more than mere official talks; it thrives on cultural exchange, diligent trust-building, and respect for sovereignty and diversity. It fundamentally demands patience and the crucial recognition that lasting solutions emerge from compromise, not coercion.

History is replete with diplomatic breakthroughs that have prevented wars, resolved conflicts, and forged alliances. Diplomacy backed by peace offers a sustainable alternative to the destructive logic of power struggles.

South Africa's transition from apartheid—a brutal system of racial segregation enforced through violence—to a democratic society stands as a landmark example of peace prevailing over power. Despite decades of oppression and conflict, the peaceful negotiation process led by visionary leaders and civil society activists dismantled apartheid.

International sanctions and global solidarity exerted pressure, but it was the commitment to dialogue, truth, and reconciliation that ultimately transformed a divided nation. The establishment of the Truth and Reconciliation Commission emphasized healing over retribution, demonstrating peace's power to unify and rebuild. The Cold War's division of Germany symbolized ideological conflict between East and West, power blocs armed to the teeth and suspicious of each other. The peaceful fall of the Berlin Wall in 1989 marked the collapse of that division, achieved not through violence but through popular protest, diplomatic shifts, and the willingness of leaders to embrace change.

German reunification followed extensive diplomatic engagement, balancing national aspirations with regional and international concerns. This process exemplified how peace, supported by persistent dialogue, can overcome entrenched divisions imposed by power politics. The decades-long conflict in Northern Ireland, characterized by sectarian violence between communities, was resolved through a complex peace process culminating in the Good Friday Agreement of 1998. This agreement, brokered with international involvement, showed how inclusive negotiations, respect for identities, and power-sharing arrangements can transform violent conflict.

The success of the peace process hinges on the unwavering commitment of political leaders and communities to dialogue and reconciliation, illustrating peace's innate ability to heal deeply rooted divisions and forge a stable political future.

The threat of nuclear annihilation during the Cold War prompted global efforts to limit and reduce nuclear weapons through treaties such as the **Non-Proliferation Treaty (NPT), Strategic Arms Reduction Treaty (START)**, and the **Intermediate-Range Nuclear Forces Treaty (INF).**

These treaties represent instances where nations prioritized global security and peace over strategic dominance, agreeing to transparency, verification, and disarmament. They underscore peace as a shared global interest, achievable only through cooperation and trust.

Countries that deploy peacekeepers to conflict zones contribute to global stability, supporting peace processes through impartial presence and humanitarian assistance. Beyond military means, soft power—through culture, education, and humanitarian aid—builds trust and fosters peace. Nations that excel in cultural diplomacy use their heritage, arts, and values as tools to connect with others, creating goodwill that sustains peace over time. **Culture is the language of the soul and a powerful catalyst for peace.** When nations share their music, literature, cuisine, and art, they create human connections that transcend political differences.

Cultural diplomacy humanizes foreign relations, breaking down stereotypes and fostering mutual respect. It encourages empathy by showcasing shared human experiences and values. International festivals, exchange programs, and global media bring diverse peoples closer, reducing fear and misunderstanding. **Sports diplomacy** also plays a vital role in peacebuilding, uniting people across divides through friendly competition and shared enthusiasm. By wisely investing in cultural diplomacy, nations build networks of trust and friendship that provide exceptionally fertile ground for peaceful cooperation and dialogue.

Peace is the undeniable foundation of sustainable development. Conflict systematically disrupts economies, displaces vast populations, destroys critical infrastructure, and depletes natural resources. Without peace, efforts to eradicate poverty, improve education, and address climate change falter. Conversely, peace enables countries to focus on long-term development goals. It attracts investment, fosters innovation, and empowers communities. **Sustainable development and peace are interdependent**: just societies with equitable growth are less prone to conflict, and peaceful environments create the conditions for sustainable progress. Global cooperation on issues such as climate action, pandemics, and migration depends on peace and trust between nations. The United Nations' **Sustainable Development Goals** explicitly link peace, justice, and strong institutions as critical to global well-being.

Beyond politics and economics, **peace profoundly heals the human spirit**. War leaves deep scars—trauma, loss, and broken communities—that endure across generations.

Peace allows healing to begin. It restores hope, enables reconciliation, and nurtures resilience. In societies recovering from conflict, peace facilitates education, mental health support, and social cohesion.

Individuals living in peace can dream, create, and contribute. Peace is, therefore, absolutely essential for psychological well-being, enabling cultures to truly thrive and societies to robustly rebuild their identities. Peace faces many challenges: nationalism, extremism, inequality, and competition for resources can inflame tensions. Geopolitical rivalries and mistrust often derail peace efforts. Overcoming these obstacles requires sustained commitment to dialogue, education that promotes empathy and critical thinking, and international frameworks that enforce justice and human rights. Civil society, youth, and women play crucial roles in peacebuilding, ensuring inclusive processes that reflect diverse voices and needs.

Technology and social media, while offering opportunities for connection, can also spread misinformation and polarization, requiring new approaches to digital peacebuilding Peace is not weakness; it is courage—the courage to choose dialogue over destruction, empathy over enmity, and justice over revenge. It is the greatest power humanity can wield, enabling progress, dignity, and shared prosperity.

In a world still fraught with uncertainty and pervasive conflict, peace lights the path toward a future where borders connect rather than divide, where children grow without fear, and where humanity's full potential is finally unleashed for the common good.

The power of peace is limitless, and it belongs to all who dare to dream and act for a better tomorrow.

COVID-19: A Test of Humanity, A Triumph of Bharat

The COVID-19 pandemic was not merely a health emergency—it was a global existential crisis that upended lives, halted economies, and tested the moral fibre of nations. For India, a country with over 1.4 billion citizens and enormous demographic diversity, the challenge was monumental. Yet, in the face of unprecedented adversity, India remarkably transformed crisis into opportunity, emerging not just as a survivor—but as a global leader in compassion, innovation, and public health resilience.

When the first case was reported in January 2020, few could foresee the devastating storm to come. By March, a nationwide lockdown—the largest in human history—was decisively imposed, impacting every village, town, and megacity. This early and bold move gave India time to strategize and mobilize its scarce resources.

India swiftly pivoted to self-reliance. PPE kits, which were being imported at the time, saw domestic production rise from virtually zero to more than 450,000 units per day within a few months. Ventilator production was scaled massively. Makeshift COVID hospitals were erected in sports arenas and railway coaches were converted into isolation wards. The Indian Railways undertook an extraordinary logistic feat, running over 4,000 'Shramik Special' trains, transporting more than 6.3 million migrant workers safely back to their hometowns.

Digital technology played a vital role. The Aarogya Setu app became one of the world's most downloaded health contact-tracing tools, and the CoWIN platform was internationally praised for enabling transparent and efficient vaccine registrations and slot allotments. With over 2 billion vaccine doses administered; India ran the largest vaccination campaign in recorded history.

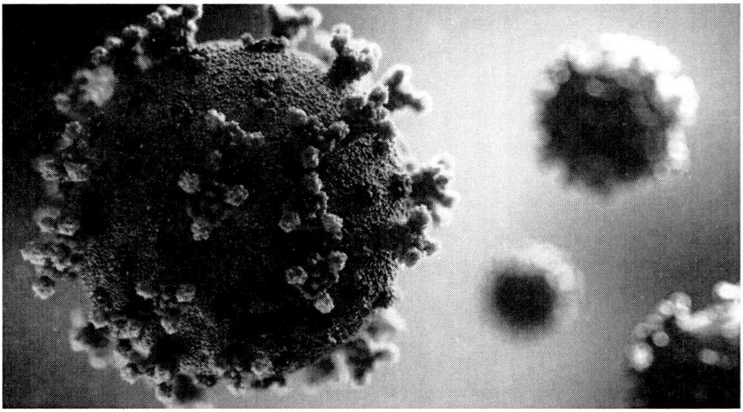

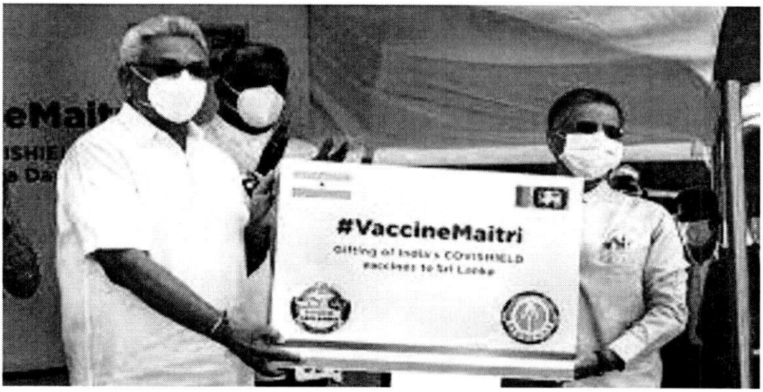

Global Solidarity in Action: *Vaccine Maitri*

While developed nations turned inward, stockpiling vaccines and medical equipment, India extended a hand. Under the *Vaccine Maitri* initiative, **India exported over 230 million doses to more than 95 countries,** including low-income and middle-income nations in Africa, South Asia, Latin America, and the Caribbean.

Despite facing its own devastating second wave in 2021, India maintained its commitment to humanitarian diplomacy. By extending help to countries like Nepal, Bhutan, Bangladesh, and the Maldives, India showcased not just capacity but also character.

International media headlines began to shift. From skepticism in the early days to admiration in later stages, **India was hailed as the "Pharmacy of the World,"** a tag it earned not through self-promotion but through life-saving action. The World Health Organization and UNICEF praised India's vaccine production and equitable distribution model.

The Role of the Armed Forces and Civil Society

India's armed forces played a crucial logistical role. The Indian Air Force airlifted oxygen tankers, ventilators, and critical medicines across states. The Navy launched ***Operation Samudra Setu II*** to transport oxygen containers from overseas suppliers during the oxygen crisis. Concurrently, civil society organizations, religious institutions, and grassroots volunteers stepped in to distribute food, provide financial assistance, and run awareness campaigns in rural and urban poor communities.

India's handling of COVID-19 was not perfect. The second wave exposed healthcare weaknesses and oxygen shortages. However, the nation responded with introspection and intensity. **Oxygen production was increased more than tenfold in 2021**, with over 1,200 PSA oxygen plants installed across hospitals through the PM CARES Fund. Rural healthcare also saw a renewed focus, with mobile medical units and **ASHA workers emerging as the backbone of the village health network.**

From Tragedy to Transformation

Every crisis offers a lesson—and India, rather than denying its shortcomings, used them as a catalyst for reform. Health infrastructure budgets were increased, and pandemic preparedness guidelines were redrafted. The **National Digital Health Mission (NDHM)** was launched to integrate data for personalized healthcare delivery. India's Biotech and Pharmaceutical sectors surged ahead, with companies like **Serum Institute of India, Bharat Biotech**, and **Biological E** gaining global acclaim.

Stories of Hope and Humanity

It wasn't just the systems—it was the people. A vegetable vendor in Bihar who donated his savings for migrant food kits. A teacher in Kerala who converted his home into a COVID care center. A Muslim man in Maharashtra who cremated over 500 Hindu COVID victims when their families could not. These are not stories of governance; they are stories of the soul of **Bharat**.

The Outcome: A Global Image Recast

In the post-pandemic world, India's stature has grown. The G20 Presidency in 2023, themed "*One Earth, One Family, One Future*", symbolized a culmination of India's pandemic-era diplomacy. India was no longer just a regional player—it became a global conscience keeper.

The **soft power** India exercised during COVID-19 was unmatched—**compassionate, calculated, and deeply cultural**. No weapons. No intimidation. Just a billion people rising together to protect their own and help the world. This wasn't just a public health victory—it was a civilizational reaffirmation of India's timeless values: **Seva (service)**, **Sahyog (cooperation)**, and **Sankalp (determination)**.

CHAPTER 3

India and Pakistan: Unfinished Chapter of Peace

Recent: Pahalgam Tragedy

India's counter-terrorism policy hinges on **zero tolerance**, **swift legal action**, and **global collaboration**. Domestically, the **Unlawful Activities (Prevention) Act** empowers agencies like the **National Investigation Agency (NIA)** and **National Security Guard (NSG)** to investigate, detain, and prosecute terrorists under strict timelines. Strategically, India reserves the right to **retaliate on its own terms**, as explified by precision strikes like **Operation Sindoor**, while simultaneously upholding**proportionality** and **rule-of-law** principles. Internationally, India leverages **UN Security Council forums**, **extradition treaties**, and initiatives like **NATGRID** to disrupt terror financing and facilitate intelligence sharing. This blend of legal deterrence, calibrated force, and multilateral diplomacy defines India's robust, rights-anchored approach to combating terrorism.

On 22 April 2025, four gunmen ambushed tourists in a meadow near Pahalgam in Jammu & Kashmir. They deliberately separated the group by religion, asking men to recite Islamic verses and shooting those who failed – predominantly Hindu men Twenty-five Indian tourists and one Nepali national were killed, with dozens more wounded.

Reuters noted this was "*the worst attack on civilians in India since the 2008 Mumbai shootings*". A shadowy group calling itself the "**Kashmir Resistance**" claimed the massacre, blaming outsiders in the valley; Indian officials immediately identified it as a front for Pakistan-backed Lashkar-e-Taiba/Hizbul militants. Pakistan's government flatly denied involvement and offered condolences for the victims

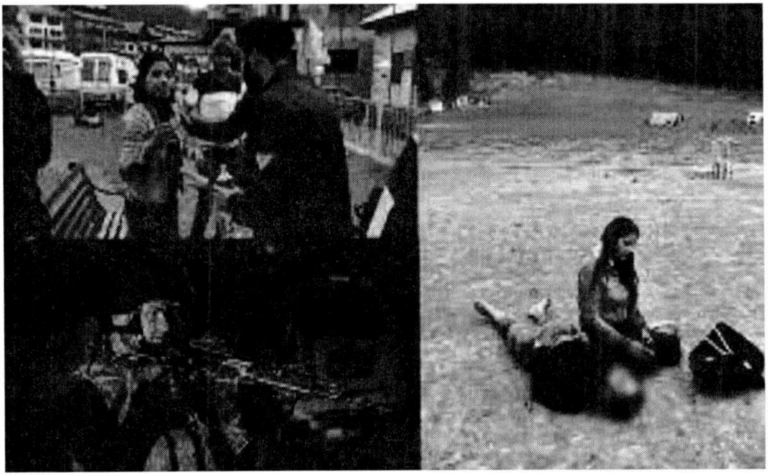

Emergency Response: The accompanying photograph (AP) depicts victims being rushed to hospital after the Pahalgam shooting. Authorities promptly locked down the area and initiated large-scale searches, but the attackers evaded capture. Kashmiri leaders expressed shock: former Chief Minister Omar Abdullah described it "*much larger than anything we've seen directed at civilians in recent years*". The massacre shattered Kashmir's fragile tourism boom which had attracted approximately 3.5 million visitors in 2024 and subsequently sparked widespread street protests.

Chronology of Key Events:

1. **22 April 2025:** Gunmen attack Pahalgam (26 dead)

2. **Late April 2025:** India mounts a security crackdown. Thousands of Kashmiris (especially young men) are detained or questioned; with dozens charged under security laws. The Indus Waters Treaty is suspended, the Wagah border crossing is sealed, and visas for Pakistani nationals are cancelled. Prime Minister Modi publicly vows to hunt down the attackers "to the ends of the earth"
3. **Late April 2025:** India launches a diplomatic offensive: External Affairs Minister Jaishankar briefs UN Security Council envoys, and India emphasizes Pakistan's alleged involvement. Pakistan denies the accusations and demands an impartial investigation.
4. **7 May 2025:** India carries out **Operation Sindoor** involving coordinated missile strikes on nine militant sites in Pakistan and Pakistan-administered Kashmir
5. **8 May 2025:** Pakistan retaliates. Its military claims to have shot down five Indian jets (a claim India rejects) and reports 31 civilians killed by Indian strikes. Pakistan simultaneously launches its own drone and missile strikes on Indian bases, all of which India states it intercepted
6. **Early May 2025:** Both sides exchange artillery and small-arms fire along the Line of Control. The U.S. and China publicly urge restraint and de-escalation. By mid-May, intense diplomatic pressure leads to a relative pause to the crisis.

Immediate Aftermath and Diplomatic Response

In response to the attack, India acted swiftly on multiple fronts, blaming Pakistan-based terrorists and imposing strict measures: **water and trade** – India suspended the Indus

Waters Treaty and halted cross-border trade; **border/visas** – the Attari-Wagah crossing was closed and Pakistani aircraft barred from Indian airspace, and visas for Pakistani nationals were cancelled (with some Pakistani diplomats expelled). **Domestic security** – Jammu & Kashmir was placed under curfew. Authorities initiated mass raids: thousands of local men were detained or questioned (approximately 90 of whom were held under the stringent Public Safety Act) and the homes of several suspected militants or their associates were demolished.

Diplomatically, India initiated global outreach. PM Modi vowed to identify and punish the culprits, and Foreign Secretary Vikram Misri briefed the media on India's planned response. India's External Affairs Minister addressed UN Security Council envoys, highlighting *"cross-border linkages"* to the attack. The United States publicly urged both India and Pakistan to *"de-escalate tensions"*, while Pakistan's Prime Minister Sharif rejected India's allegations and asked the US to press India to *"dial down the rhetoric."* Pakistan, for its part, flatly denied any state role (asserting it offers only moral, not material, support to Kashmiri insurgents), but warned that any Indian incursion would be answered forcefully.

India's measures (Indus Treaty suspension, border closures, etc.) delivered both a symbolic message and a practical blow. A government release later justified the treaty suspension by stating *"blood and water cannot flow together"*, implying that support for terrorism nullifies normal treaties. These steps marked a clear escalation from previous crises: analysts observed that unlike earlier attacks (e.g. Uri 2016, Pulwama 2019, which primarily targeted soldiers), the Pahalgam attack specifically targeted Hindu civilians much like the 2008

Mumbai massacre, thereby prompting an unusually forceful Indian posture.

Operation Sindoor (India's Retaliatory Strikes, 7 May 2025)

On 7 May 2025 (15 days after the Pahalgam attack), India announced a bold counterstrike code-named **Operation Sindoor**. Using precision-guided missiles, Indian forces hit nine terror-related sites in Pakistan and Pakistan-administered Kashmir. Official statements said the targets were militant infrastructure – for example, a *Lashkar-e-Taiba* training camp and mosque in Bahawalpur, and a training center in Muridke – deliberately chosen to avoid Pakistan's regular military bases. Satellite imagery (Maxar) later confirmed extensive damage at these sites

India's government portrayed the strikes as *"measured and proportionate"* retribution aimed only at those behind the terror attack. Pakistani media reported that 31 civilians died in the strikes. India, however, insisted all targets were terrorist safe havens, not Pakistani army positions. (For example, India's

Defence Minister said the strikes were precise and "unimaginable" in execution, emphasizing no Indian soldier was lost and no civilian Pakistani lives were targeted.) Satellite images and journalism support the official account that militant camps - including the Muridke mosque seen above - were hit.

Pakistan's Counteraction and Escalation

Pakistan immediately vowed retaliation. Its military spokesman asserted that Pakistan had shot down five Indian fighters during the exchanges, a claim India categorically denied, reporting no loss of aircraft. In the day following Operation Sindoor, artillery and rockets flew across the Line of Control: Pakistan shelled border towns in Jammu, and India returned fire. Pakistan reported that dozens of its civilians were killed by the Indian strikes, while India stated that at least 15 of its own civilians were killed in the Pakistani shelling.

On 8 May, Pakistani forces reportedly launched unmanned drones and missile salvos toward Indian military installations including bases in Jammu and Himachal Pradesh. Indian officials stated they successfully shot down the Pakistani drone (using an S-400 system) and intercepted the incoming missiles. This tit-for-tat marked "*the worst clash in more than two decades*" between the nuclear-armed rivals. Internationally, both governments faced significant pressure: the U.S. and UN urged restrain, and China, a key ally of Pakistan, formally "hoped for restraint" from both sides. Both sides halted major new strikes by mid-May, likely deterred by the palpable risk of a wider war and the potential for global outcry.

Operation Sindoor: Fact vs Fiction

In the ensuing weeks, Operation Sindoor became the subject of intense information warfare. Pakistani media and social media platforms circulated claims that Sindoor was a hoax or that India had suffered heavy losses. For example, social media posts alleged Pakistani forces shot down Indian Rafale jets or attacked Srinagar airbase – stories India's Press Information Bureau quickly labeled "Pakistan-sponsored propaganda. PIB fact-checkers debunked viral images, clarifying that a widely shared photo of a crashed jet was from an unrelated 2019 accident.

Independent outlets, however, treated Operation Sindoor as a genuine event. Al Jazeera and BBC confirmed that on 7 May *"India struck multiple targets in Pakistan… in the aftermath of the Pahalgam attack"*, explicitly noting the codename Operation Sindoor. Reputable reports cited ISPR's casualty figures and India's own statements. Satellite images provided tangible evidence of damaged camps. In sum, cross-referencing sources shows Operation Sindoor was an actual military action (the official codename for the strikes), not merely symbolic. Misinformation swirled, but authoritative sources and imagery confirm it occured essentially as India described.

Strategic Impact and Geopolitical Context

The Pahalgam incident and its aftermath reaffirmed India's hardening stance toward cross-border terrorism. Indian officials framed the retaliatory strike as defining a "new red line" – declaring that if terror is a state policy, it will be met with visible and forceful response. By combining military action with economic and diplomatic leverage (suspending the Indus Water Treaty and trade), India conveyed a strategic message of zero tolerance. Critics noted this moves India away from restraint: using water diplomacy as a punitive tool ("blood and water cannot flow together") and explicitly threatening further consequences if Pakistan is implicated.

However, the crisis also underscored the limits imposed by nuclear deterrence. Neither side sought full-scale war. After a brief spike in tensions, global powers (notably the U.S. and China) urged both capitals to de-escalate, as reflected in their public calls for calm. Islamabad's denials of involvement garnered it some diplomatic cover (Pakistan's campaign emphasized external conspiracy and accused India of propaganda), whereas India's narrative gained traction among nations committed to countering terrorism. Analysts compared the episode to past crises: it blended aspects of the Mumbai (2008) and Pulwama (2019) attacks, but culminated in a more overt military reprisal.

In the broader geopolitical setting, the flare-up has reinforced the chronic instability of the Kashmir dispute. Each new attack triggers a cycle of tit-for-tat brinkmanship. For decades, India and Pakistan have fought wars and waged insurgencies over Kashmir, and this event regrettably fits that pattern. Going forward, the Pahalgam–Sindoor episode is likely to significantly influence South Asian strategy: India appears resolute in linking counterterrorism tightly to its foreign policy, while Pakistan will undoubtedly face increased international scrutiny over any militants operating on its soil. Bilateral relations remain severely strained, with traditional confidence-building measures such as trade or cultural exchange now sidelined. The crisis thus serves as a compelling case study in how terrorism, nationalism, and nuclear realities intertwine in Indo-Pak diplomacy.

Lapses Behind Pahalgam Tragedy

Intelligence Breakdown: Early Alerts, Late Actions

Multiple intelligence alerts were issued in the weeks leading up to the attack. As per internal assessments cited by *The New Indian Express* (April 2025), central agencies had intercepted communications hinting at planned attacks in the tourist-heavy Anantnag region. Further investigation later revealed that LeT operatives had surveyed hotels in Pahalgam weeks before the attack. However, these alerts remained either under-assessed or were not escalated effectively to ground-level security forces.

India's intelligence infrastructure, though expansive, faces a coordination lag between central and state actors. The Multi-Agency Centre (MAC), meant to integrate inputs from agencies like IB, R&AW, NIA, and NTRO, has often suffered from inter-agency silos and lack of actionable follow-through. This systemic issue requires structural overhaul.

Procedural Oversight: Unauthorized Opening of Baisaran

One of the most serious lapses identified was the premature opening of the Baisaran meadow to tourists. Traditionally restricted until the annual Amarnath Yatra in June, Baisaran was opened in April 2025 without proper coordination with the Ministry of Home Affairs or the Armed Forces Special Powers Act (AFSPA)-authorized security deployments. This move not only contravened standard security protocols but also exposed unprepared terrain to a mass civilian presence.

This decision, allegedly driven by local tourism bodies and supported by state administrators aiming to boost the economy, lacked adequate security clearance. In a conflict-sensitive zone like Kashmir, such decisions must be thoroughly vetted by unified command structures under the Unified Headquarters mechanism.

Infrastructure Failures: A Valley Left Unwatched

Despite being a high-footfall location, Baisaran lacked basic surveillance infrastructure. There were no CCTV cameras, aerial drone coverage, or mobile jamming systems in place. Given that Pahalgam is categorized under Zone II of the Ministry of Home Affairs' Vulnerability Index for terrorism, this lack of technological safeguards is alarming.

The Communications Ministry had earlier proposed a plan in 2023 for the installation of drone-based monitoring in high-risk zones. However, budgetary constraints and procurement delays under the Digital Surveillance Expansion Plan (DSEP) left the region unmonitored during the critical window.

And in the conclusion, it is clear **that a place having 1000+ visitors daily should not have been left unguarded.**

Operational Delay: Terrain and Response Limitations

The terrain of Baisaran—a high-altitude meadow accessible only via foot or pony—is both a logistical challenge and a strategic vulnerability. It took over 60 minutes for the CRPF Quick Reaction Team to reach the attack site, during which local pony handlers and civilians undertook rescue efforts with no medical support.

While the CRPF is equipped for riot control and basic tactical response, the lack of immediate airlift capabilities in such terrains severely limits their efficiency. Recommendations made post the 2017 Amarnath attack for heli-rescue systems and rapid evacuation infrastructure were partially implemented but not extended to all high-risk zones.

Overconfidence in Normalcy: The Strategic Complacency

Over the past few years, the government narrative emphasized a return to normalcy in Jammu & Kashmir. Increased tourist influx and reduced stone-pelting incidents fed a belief that terrorism had receded in intensity. However, this perception resulted in an underestimation of residual terror networks operating from across the Line of Control (LoC).

Statements from senior government officials in early 2025 had described Kashmir as being in its "*most peaceful decade*." However, as per Ministry of Defence figures, **infiltration attempts had seen a 14% rise from Q3 2024 to Q1 2025**, suggesting a more volatile ground reality than publicly acknowledged.

Lack of Clear SOPs for High-Density Civilian Zones

Post-attack evaluations revealed that no clear Standard Operating Procedure (SOP) existed for mass-casualty response in Pahalgam. Who takes operational lead? Who coordinates civilian evacuation? How are medical supplies routed? These basic questions had no ready answers during the crisis.

While India's **National Disaster Management Authority (NDMA)** guidelines exist, they were not adequately drilled or localized for the region. The absence of mock drills, community safety training, and a dedicated crisis response command for high-altitude zones remains a glaring flaw.

And once again, a haunting question resurfaces — '*how did these terrorists infiltrate across the Line of Control despite constant surveillance by the Border Security Forces?*' More critically, '*where did they vanish post-attack? Was there local assistance in their swift escape and possible evacuation?*'

Recommendations and The Road Ahead

Rather than seeking scapegoats, the path forward requires serious systemic reform:

- Strengthen Intelligence Integration: Establish a Kashmir-specific Intelligence Fusion Centre to synchronize state and central alerts.
- Mandate Inter-Agency Drills: Conduct quarterly joint drills in all high-risk zones, involving army, CRPF, local police, and health services.
- Upgrade Surveillance: Implement Phase-II of DSEP with urgent funding, prioritizing Pahalgam, Gulmarg, and Sonmarg.
- Civil-Military Coordination: Empower Unified Command structures to approve all tourism openings.
- Terrain-Specific Response Units: Deploy pony-mounted or ATV-equipped rapid forces in terrain-inaccessible areas.

Conclusion: From Retaliation to Resilience

The nation responded with might and precision through Operation Sindoor. But true strength lies not in how we retaliate—but in how we prevent. Pahalgam must become the last chapter of such horror. Let this loss teach us not only how to avenge—but how to protect, prepare, and prevail. Our tears must fuel our transformation.

The Mirage of Falsehood: Pakistan's Fabricated Accusations Against India

In the complex theatre of South Asian geopolitics, truth often becomes a casualty, overshadowed by narratives woven to serve strategic ends. Pakistan's long-standing campaign of false accusations against India forms a disturbing chapter in this saga—one where misinformation, deliberate distortions, and unsubstantiated claims have been systematically employed to deflect attention from Pakistan's own role in fostering instability and terrorism in the region.

At the heart of Pakistan's global narrative lies the persistent, yet baseless, allegation that India is the primary aggressor in Jammu & Kashmir and a violator of human rights. This rhetoric is frequently echoed in diplomatic corridors, international forums, and media outlets, painting India as an oppressor and Pakistan as the victim. However, a closer scrutiny of facts, documented evidence, and independent reports reveals a starkly different reality—one that dismantles these claims with undeniable clarity.

Pakistan's accusations often cite alleged "*excessive use of force*" by Indian security forces in Kashmir, a charge repeatedly amplified to gain international sympathy and support. Yet, reports from neutral organizations such as the **United Nations Human Rights Council (UNHRC)** and **Amnesty International** have consistently highlighted the role of Pakistan-backed terrorist groups in perpetuating violence and destabilizing the region. The narrative conveniently omits the orchestrated infiltration attempts, cross-border shelling, and terror strikes launched from Pakistan-administered territories—actions documented by India's Ministry of Defence and international security analysts alike.

Moreover, Pakistan's portrayal of Kashmir as a "freedom struggle" front obscures the voices of the majority Kashmiri population who, despite challenges, have repeatedly expressed a desire for peace and development within the Indian constitutional framework. The political processes—state elections, peace dialogues, and socio-economic reforms—spearheaded by India since 2014 underscore this reality. Pakistan's false narrative ignores these democratic exercises, choosing instead to spotlight isolated incidents to malign India's reputation.

The international community has also witnessed Pakistan's strategic manipulation of terror attacks to shift blame onto India. For instance, attacks such as the **2016 Uri** and the **2019 Pulwama Attack**, both orchestrated by Pakistan-based groups, were cynically met with Pakistani denials and counter-accusations. Islamabad's attempts to use its propaganda machinery to portray these acts of terror as internal Indian conflicts seek to muddy waters and evade responsibility. In contrast, India has consistently provided detailed evidence—through captured terrorists' confessions, intercepted communications, and international intelligence cooperation—that link these attacks directly to Pakistani terror infrastructure.

Biggest Question Arises- ***Why were Pakistani Military Generals present at the funerals of terrorists?***

Pakistan's use of international platforms like the **United Nations, Organization of Islamic Cooperation (OIC)**, and global media is marked by repetition of these unverified claims, designed to create diplomatic pressure on India. Yet, many countries have recognized this pattern and approached such accusations with caution. Independent observers and analysts often warn against the simplistic narrative promoted by Pakistan, emphasizing the need to address terrorism at its source rather than rewarding false victimhood.

An important facet of Pakistan's misinformation campaign is its denial or minimization of its own internal human rights abuses, particularly in Balochistan and Gilgit-Baltistan—regions where dissent is met with harsh crackdowns. This selective narrative highlights a troubling hypocrisy: while accusing India of violations, Pakistan consistently suppresses its own citizens' voices and freedoms. International human rights reports from **Amnesty International** and **Human Rights Watch** have repeatedly condemned Pakistan for extrajudicial killings, enforced disappearances, and suppression of free expression in these regions.

Furthermore, Pakistan's international posturing attempts to divert attention from its role as a sanctuary for terrorist groups, including ***Lashkar-e-Taiba, Jaish-e-Mohammed,*** and the ***Haqqani* network**. These organizations have been designated as terrorist entities by multiple countries, including the **United States**, the **United Kingdom**, and the **United Nations Security Council**. Yet, Pakistan continues to deny or downplay these links, presenting itself as a victim rather than a perpetrator. This duplicity undermines regional peace efforts and complicates India's efforts to foster a peaceful and stable neighborhood.

Diplomatically, India's response has been firm yet measured—focused on evidence-based dialogue, strategic counter-terrorism operations, and expanding global partnerships. India's proactive sharing of intelligence, raising terrorism as a global concern, and its emphasis on development diplomacy in Kashmir demonstrate a commitment to peace, contrasting sharply with Pakistan's blame game.

In conclusion, Pakistan's false accusations against India represent a deliberate attempt to rewrite reality, evade responsibility, and internationalize a bilateral dispute in ways that hinder genuine resolution. These fabrications, while rhetorically powerful, crumble under the weight of documented facts and strategic realities. The world must recognize that true peace in South Asia will come not from manufactured narratives, but from confronting uncomfortable truths, dismantling terror networks, and fostering genuine dialogue based on mutual respect and factual clarity.

Pakistan IMF Loan: Terror Fundings?

In May 2025, the **International Monetary Fund** approved the disbursement of approximately $1 billion to Pakistan under its ongoing **Extended Fund Facility (EFF)**, bringing total disbursements to about $2.1 billion. This financial assistance, while aimed at stabilizing Pakistan's faltering economy, comes with stringent conditions. The IMF imposed 11 new conditions, raising the total to 50, focusing on fiscal reforms, energy sector restructuring, and governance improvements. Notably, the IMF has expressed concerns over rising tensions between Pakistan and India, warning that such geopolitical strains could heighten risks to the fiscal, external, and reform goals of the program. This highlights the interconnectedness of regional stability and economic reform efforts.

Critics argue that despite these conditions, there remains a lack of transparency in how Pakistan allocates these funds. Concerns have been raised about the potential diversion of financial aid towards activities that may not align with the intended purpose of economic stabilization and development. Indian Defence Minister Rajnath Singh has voiced apprehensions that such aid could inadvertently fund activities detrimental to regional security.

The IMF's decision to continue financial support, despite these concerns, underscores the complexities of international financial assistance in geopolitically sensitive regions. It raises critical questions about the mechanisms in place to ensure that such funds are utilized appropriately and do not inadvertently exacerbate regional tensions.

This situation calls for a more robust framework for monitoring and accountability, ensuring that financial aid fulfills its intended purpose of fostering economic stability and development, without unintended consequences.

The Paradox of Pakistan's Counterterrorism Stance: A Critical Examination

Pakistan has long positioned itself as a frontline state in the global fight against terrorism, often highlighting the sacrifices of its military and civilian population. However, a closer examination reveals a series of contradictions that challenge this narrative. The juxtaposition of Pakistan's professed commitment to counterterrorism with its actions—ranging from harboring high-profile terrorists to political patronage of extremist groups—raises critical questions about its true intentions and the efficacy of its counterterrorism efforts.

Harboring High-Profile Terrorists

One of the most glaring contradictions is Pakistan's harboring of Osama Bin Laden, the mastermind behind the September 11 attacks. Bin Laden was found and killed in 2011 in a fortified compound in Abbottabad, merely 1.3 kilometers from the Pakistan Military Academy in Kakul. The proximity of his residence to a major military installation raises serious doubts about Pakistan's claims of ignorance regarding his whereabouts.

Further complicating matters, investigative reports suggest that Pakistan's Inter-Services Intelligence (ISI) may have been aware of Osama Bin Laden's presence. A retired Pakistani general reportedly stated that the ISI kept Laden in Abbottabad to maintain control over him and to use him as leverage in dealings with **Al-Qaeda** and the **Taliban**.

Political Patronage of Designated Terrorists

Pakistan's political landscape has also been marred by the patronage of individuals and groups designated as terrorists by international bodies. **Masood Azhar**, the **founder of Jaish-e-Mohammed (JeM)**, has been a focal point in this regard. Despite being listed under the **United Nations Security Council Resolution 1267**, Azhar has operated with relative impunity within Pakistan.

Efforts to sanction Azhar have been repeatedly blocked by China, Pakistan's close ally, citing insufficient evidence. This obstruction has allowed Azhar and JeM to continue their operations, including the 2019 Pulwama attack that killed 40 Indian paramilitary personnel.

Military and Intelligence Complicity

The complicity of Pakistan's military and intelligence agencies in supporting terrorist groups has been a subject of international concern. Leaked diplomatic cables and intelligence reports have indicated that elements within the ISI have provided support to militant groups operating in Afghanistan and India.

Moreover, the presence of jihadi training camps in regions like Khyber Pakhtunkhwa and Balochistan, areas under tight military control, suggests a level of institutional support or, at the very least, willful negligence.

Public Displays of Support

Pakistan's duplicity is further evidenced by public displays of support for individuals associated with terrorism. High-ranking military officials have been reported to attend funerals of militants, lending an air of legitimacy to their actions. Such events not only embolden extremist elements but also undermine Pakistan's stated commitment to combating terrorism.

International Implications and the Need for Accountability

Pakistan's contradictory stance has significant implications for regional and global security. Its actions have not only destabilized neighboring countries but have also strained its relationships with international partners. The United States, for instance, has expressed frustration over Pakistan's failure to take decisive action against terrorist groups operating within its borders.

Given these concerns, there is a pressing need for the international community to hold Pakistan accountable. This includes reevaluating military and economic aid, imposing targeted sanctions, and increasing diplomatic pressure to ensure compliance with international counterterrorism norms.

Global Response to the Pahalgam Tragedy

International Condemnation and Calls for Restraint

The Pahalgam terrorist attack on April 22, 2025, which resulted in the deaths of 26 civilians, has elicited widespread international condemnation and concern. Nations across the globe have expressed solidarity with India, denounced the act of terror, and urged both India and Pakistan to exercise restraint to prevent further escalation.e

United Nations and International Organizations

United Nations Secretary-General António Guterres condemned the Pahalgam attack and expressed deep concern over the escalating tensions between India and Pakistan. He emphasized that a military solution is not viable and called for peaceful dialogue between the two nations. Guterres offered the support of the UN to facilitate efforts aimed at restoring calm and fostering cooperation between India and Pakistan.

The **United Nations Security Council (UNSC)** also held emergency closed consultations to discuss the situation. The press statement from the UNSC condemned the terrorist attack in Jammu and Kashmir in the strongest terms and reaffirmed that *"terrorism in all its forms and manifestations* *constitutes one of the most serious threats to international peace and security".*

United States

The United States strongly condemned the Pahalgam attack and expressed support for India's counterterrorism efforts. The U.S. State Department updated its travel advisory, issuing a Level 4 "Do Not Travel" warning for India's Jammu and Kashmir region, citing high risks of terrorism and civil unrest. Additionally, the U.S. Embassy in New Delhi confirmed it is closely monitoring the situation and called for the perpetrators to be brought to justice. In the wake of escalating tensions, U.S. Secretary of State Marco Rubio engaged in extensive diplomacy with Indian and Pakistani officials, ultimately brokering a ceasefire agreement. President Donald Trump announced the cessation of hostilities on social media, praising both nations for their restraint and decision to de-escalate.

European Union and United Kingdom

The European Union and the United Kingdom both issued statements condemning the Pahalgam terrorist attack and called for restraint from both India and Pakistan. The UK reiterated its longstanding position that the dispute over Kashmir is bilateral and can only be solved through negotiations by both sides, taking into account the wishes of the Kashmiri people. The UK was also reported to have been involved in discussions between India and Pakistan that led to the ceasefire

Japan

Japan's Chief Cabinet Secretary Yoshimasa Hayashi condemned the terrorist act in Kashmir and expressed strong concern that the situation may lead to further retaliatory exchanges and escalate into a full-scale military conflict. He urged both India and Pakistan to exercise restraint and stabilize the situation through dialogue for the peace and stability of South Asia.

Other Nations

Several other countries, including Iran, Israel, Italy, Saudi Arabia, the United Arab Emirates, the United Kingdom, the United States, and India's neighbors such as Afghanistan, Bangladesh, Bhutan, China, Pakistan, and Sri Lanka, issued statements condemning the attack and expressing condolences to the victims. The United States Commission on International Religious Freedom (USCIRF) also condemned the Pahalgam attack, stating concern over the explicit targeting of Hindus and other non-Muslims.

Global Protests and Diaspora Response

The Pahalgam attack sparked worldwide demonstrations, particularly among the Indian diaspora. Peaceful rallies and prayer meetings were held across the globe to express solidarity with the victims. In Delhi, over 500 people protested near the Pakistan High Commission. In the United States, members of the Indian diaspora held peaceful demonstrations in memory of the Pahalgam attack victims. The global response to the Pahalgam tragedy underscores the international community's condemnation of terrorism and its commitment to regional stability in South Asia. While there is a unanimous call for justice for the victims, there is also a concerted effort to prevent further escalation between India and Pakistan. The emphasis on dialogue and restraint reflects a collective desire to resolve disputes through peaceful means and uphold international peace and security.

This heinous act of terror in Pahalgam is not just an attack on innocent lives—it is a crime against humanity itself. Mothers lost their children, fathers lost their sons, and communities were shattered in an instant. Such brutality pierces the very soul of humanity, reminding us all that hatred and violence spare no one and devastate all. To the global community, this is a solemn call: terrorism anywhere is a threat everywhere. We must rise together—not just in words, but in unified action—to protect human dignity, preserve peace, and ensure that such darkness never again engulfs the light of innocent lives. Silence or indifference is complicity; let compassion and justice guide us all.

Media Misguidance and Its Impact on Public Perception During the Pahalgam Tragedy

The tragic events in Pahalgam sent shockwaves across the nation, capturing intense media attention that shaped how millions perceived not only the tragedy but also the broader Kashmir conflict. In such critical moments, the media's responsibility extends beyond simple reporting—it must contextualize, humanize, and foster informed understanding. However, the media's handling of the Pahalgam tragedy was marred by sensationalism, bias, and lapses in journalistic ethics, which ultimately misled the public and exacerbated an already fragile situation.

One of the most damaging aspects of media coverage was the sensationalist approach adopted by many outlets. Graphic images and emotionally charged language dominated headlines and news bulletins, often repeated excessively without adequate sensitivity or warnings. This not only turned profound human suffering into a spectacle but also reduced the multifaceted Kashmir conflict to a simplistic narrative of "*terrorists versus innocent civilians*." The urgency to capture viewer attention and boost ratings overshadowed the need for nuanced reporting that acknowledged the deep-rooted political, social, and historical complexities behind the violence.

Equally troubling was the media's frequent selective reporting and partisan framing. Different outlets pushed contrasting narratives shaped by ideological biases or political pressures. Some framed the tragedy solely as a breach of national security, glorifying the state's military response and downplaying civilian grievances. Others emphasized Kashmiri victimhood without adequately addressing the actions of militant groups, fostering an incomplete and polarized public discourse. This fragmentation sowed confusion and mistrust among citizens, as each consumed vastly different versions of "truth," deepening communal and regional divides.

A critical and often overlooked failure was the media's inadvertent compromise of security operations. During the live coverage of the tragedy and subsequent army movements, many television channels broadcast real-time visuals and updates of military deployments and strategies. This unprecedented live exposure effectively handed the attackers vital tactical information, enabling them to evade security cordons or adjust their operations. Such lapses not only endangered lives on the ground but also highlighted the dangerous consequences of prioritizing breaking news over operational security. It exposed the urgent need for media outlets to balance transparency with responsibility, especially in sensitive conflict zones.

Moreover, the rush to break news led to widespread dissemination of unverified information and rumors. Casualty figures, identities, and claims of responsibility were frequently reported without confirmation, sometimes outright fabricated. This misinformation, amplified further by social media platforms, inflamed public anxiety and hostility, occasionally targeting innocent communities or stoking retaliatory sentiments. The result was a misinformed public environment that hampered peace-building and reconciliation efforts, as false narratives hardened entrenched views and obscured facts.

Beyond immediate reporting, the media largely failed to sustain attention on the long-term humanitarian impact. Once the immediate crisis passed, there was scant coverage of victims' rehabilitation, psychological trauma, or the socio-economic disruption experienced by local communities dependent on tourism and agriculture. This lack of follow-through deprived victims of continued public empathy and muted critical scrutiny of government relief efforts, allowing systemic issues that contribute to such tragedies to remain unaddressed.

The media's misguidance also had profound political repercussions. Politicians and security forces often cited media narratives to justify escalated military responses and stricter security measures in Kashmir, sometimes at the expense of civil rights. Meanwhile, opposition voices accused mainstream media of complicity with official propaganda, deepening the divide between the public and state institutions. This tug-of-war over narrative ownership undermined trust -a vital ingredient for any meaningful dialogue or conflict resolution.

Furthermore, the Pahalgam tragedy laid bare structural weaknesses in Indian journalism concerning conflict reporting. Many journalists lacked adequate training on the sensitivities of covering militancy and communal violence, frequently resorting to nationalist rhetoric without critical inquiry. Safety concerns limited on-ground reportage in Kashmir, making the media heavily reliant on official sources and vulnerable to state influence. This dependence weakened independent journalism's role as a watchdog and educator during crises.

However, these shortcomings sparked some introspection within the media industry. The tragedy underscored the necessity for ethical standards tailored to conflict zones—emphasizing fact-checking, contextual depth, survivor voices, and trauma-sensitive reporting. Digital platforms emerged as spaces for diverse, grassroots perspectives, though these also present challenges in managing misinformation. The Pahalgam incident thus became a case study in the perils and responsibilities of journalism in conflict-affected regions.

In conclusion, the media's failure to provide balanced, accurate, and sensitive coverage during the Pahalgam tragedy not only distorted public perception but also inadvertently aided militant attackers by revealing critical military movements on live television. This, combined with sensationalism, selective narratives, and misinformation, worsened communal tensions and complicated peace efforts. The episode starkly illustrates the power and peril of media narratives in conflict zones and underscores the urgent need for a responsible, ethical, and context-aware media landscape—one that serves not only to inform but also to heal.

History of India and Pakistan

Since their partition in 1947, India and Pakistan have engaged in multiple wars (1947–48, 1965, 1971, 1999) and numerous border skirmishes centered primarily on the disputed region of Jammu and Kashmir. Foundational treaties and accords—the **1949 Karachi Agreement, the 1966 Tashkent Declaration, the 1972 Simla Agreement, the 1960 Indus Waters Treaty**, and **the 1999 Lahore Declaration**—have sought to establish cease-fires, define borders, and foster cooperation but have frequently been undermined by renewed hostilities, divergent interpretations, and geopolitical pressures. While these pacts have provided frameworks for dialogue and conflict management, persistent mistrust, tactical missteps, and external influences have perpetuated a volatile relationship that continues to shape South Asian security dynamics.

British Rule and the Roots of Partition

From 1858 until 1947, the British Raj governed the Indian subcontinent, integrating diverse regions under a single colonial administration. Growing demands for self-rule and communal tensions led to Britain's Parliament passing the **Indian Independence Act in July 1947**, which mandated the division of British India into two independent dominions—India and Pakistan—by midnight of August 14–15, 1947. The rapid partition triggered one of history's largest population transfers—approximately 15 million people migrated across hastily drawn borders—and unleashed communal violence that left upwards of one million dead.

The First Indo-Pakistani War (1947–48) and the Karachi Agreement

Almost immediately after partition, the conflict over Jammu and Kashmir erupted into full-scale war in October 1947, following Pakistani tribal militias' incursion into the princely state of Kashmir. In January 1949, under UN auspices, India and Pakistan agreed to a cease-fire line—later known as the **Line of Control (LoC)**—through the **Karachi Agreement**, establishing an 830 km demarcation from near the Chenab River northwards to NJ9842. This agreement froze front-line positions but left the final status of Kashmir unresolved, sowing the seeds for future wars and enduring territorial disputes.

The Second War (1965) and the Tashkent Declaration

In August 1965, Pakistan launched **Operation Gibraltar**—sending troops across the 1949 cease-fire line aiming to incite rebellion in Kashmir—triggering India's full-scale military response, including incursions into Pakistani Punjab. The conflict lasted until the UN-brokered cease-fire on September 22, 1965, after which diplomatic efforts culminated in the **Tashkent Declaration** (January 10, 1966). Under this accord, India's Prime Minister Lal Bahadur Shastri and Pakistan's President Ayub Khan agreed to withdraw forces to pre-August 5, 1965 positions, respect non-interference in internal affairs, and resume peaceful relations.

The Third War (1971), Bangladesh Liberation, and the Simla Agreement

The 1971 war began on December 3 when Pakistan launched **Operation Chengiz Khan** against India, aiming to preemptively strike Indian air bases. India's subsequent military intervention supported Bengali nationalists (**Mukti Bahini**) in East Pakistan, leading to a swift campaign that resulted in Pakistan's surrender on December 16, 1971, and the birth of Bangladesh as an independent nation. In the war's aftermath, India and Pakistan signed the **Simla Agreement** on July 2, 1972, where both sides committed to respecting the LoC, resolving disputes through bilateral negotiations, and refraining from the use of force.

The Kargil Conflict (1999) and the Lahore Declaration

Despite the Simla framework, cross-LoC incursions persisted. In May 1999, Pakistani forces and militants occupied high-altitude posts in the Kargil sector of Kashmir, leading to a limited but intense conflict that lasted until July 1999, known as the Kargil War. The intervention of international pressure, particularly from the United States, and India's military successes forced Pakistan to withdraw its forces. Earlier that year in February, **Indian Prime Minister Atal Bihari Vajpayee** and **Pakistani Prime Minister Nawaz Sharif** had signed the **Lahore Declaration**, reaffirming commitment to the UN Charter, the Simla Agreement, and a vision of peace—only for Pakistan to violate it by initiating the Kargil infiltration.

Water Diplomacy: The Indus Waters Treaty (1960) and Its Strains

Well before the 1971 war, India and Pakistan negotiated the Indus Waters Treaty under World Bank mediation, signed on September 19, 1960. The accord allocated the three eastern rivers (Ravi, Beas, Sutlej) to India and the three western rivers (Indus, Jhelum, Chenab) to Pakistan, while granting each country limited uses on the other's rivers. Despite subsequent wars, the treaty endured as a rare example of functional cooperation. However, recent tensions following devastating attacks have led India to suspend its participation and consider major water-diversion projects that could significantly reduce Pakistan's agricultural water supply—moves Islamabad deems tantamount to war.

Despite multiple treaties aiming to resolve or manage conflicts, a pattern emerges of accords followed by renewed hostilities. The Karachi Agreement established a cease-fire but left Kashmir's fate undecided. The Tashkent and Simla agreements secured temporary peace but lacked effective enforcement mechanisms. The **Indus Waters Treaty**, while robust, is now under unprecedented stress. The **Lahore Declaration's** goodwill was quickly eclipsed by the Kargil crisis. These cycles reveal the limits of bilateral diplomacy absent third-party guarantees or confidence-building measures.

Conclusion

The India–Pakistan relationship has been shaped by colonial legacies, competing nationalisms, and strategic rivalries manifested in four full-scale wars, endless border tensions, and contested water resources. Treaties have provided frameworks for dialogue, but their recurrent breaches highlight profound trust deficits. Going forward, sustainable peace will require not only rigorous treaty enforcement and enhanced confidence-building but also broader regional cooperation—potentially involving third-party mediation or multilateral mechanisms—to transcend the zero-sum paradigm that has long defined Indo-Pakistani Interactions.

The 2025 **Global Terrorism Index** (GTI) identifies Pakistan as the **second-most terrorism-affected country** globally, with terrorism-related fatalities rising by 45% and the number of attacks more than doubling over the previous year. This surge is linked to the resurgence of ***Tehreek-e-Taliban Pakistan* (TTP)** and ongoing operations by ***Lashkar-e-Taiba* (LeT)** and ***Jaish-e-Mohammed* (JeM)** in sanctuaries along the Afghan border, illustrating both blowback from past proxy strategies and Islamabad's weakened monopoly over militant networks. Only Iraq leads Pakistan in GTI impact, underscoring the severity of terrorism's toll on Pakistani society.

Pakistan officially proscribes numerous organizations under its **Anti-Terrorism Act**, yet many—most notably LeT, JeM, and TTP—operate covertly with documented ISI backing as *"strategic assets"* against India. Major attacks on Indian soil, including the 2008 Mumbai siege, the 2016 Uri strike, and the 2019 Pulwama bombing, have all been traced to Pakistani-based training camps and handlers within the ISI, providing incontrovertible proof of state sponsorship. Beyond India-focused proxies, Pakistan's tribal areas and Balochistan serve as safe havens for transnational extremist groups—ranging from Al-Qa'ida to Central Asian separatists—making the country a regional terrorism hub.

Pakistan's international metrics paint a stark picture of chronic instability and insecurity: it ranks 140th out of 163 on the 2024 Global Peace Index with a low score of 2.783, placing it alongside active conflict zones; it is the second-most terrorism-affected country in the 2025 Global Terrorism Index, with a 45% rise in fatalities and more than double the number of attacks year-on-year; it continues to harbour and enable proscribed groups such as *Lashkar-e-Taiba, Jaish-e-Mohammed,* and *Tehreek-e-Taliban Pakistan,* whose activities have transformed its tribal areas and Balochistan into regional terror hubs; socially, it ranks 108th out of 146 in the 2024 World

Happiness Report with a life-satisfaction score of 4.657, reflecting widespread economic hardship and insecurity despite cultural resilience; and although it exited the FATF "grey list" in October 2022 after partial reforms, it remains under close monitoring for persistent deficiencies in counter-terrorist financing measures.

India and **Pakistan** have fought wars. We have buried soldiers, civilians, and stories that never got a chance. But there is a deeper truth: we've also shared songs, languages, love, and legacies. Peace is not naivety — it is the most strategic choice a brave nation can make. ***The real victory lies not in conquering each other's land, but in winning over each other's hearts***. Let's not wait for another Pulwama or another Peshawar to remind us that blood is always red, and grief sounds the same in every mother's cry. ***Let peace not just be a truce. Let it be our tribute to the generations that deserve better.***

Question of China

India and China—two ancient civilizations rising as 21st-century giants—are bound by a shared legacy of cultural exchange, yet remain deeply entangled in modern-day rivalry. Historically, the relationship wasn't born out of conflict. In fact, it began with philosophy, not politics. From the 1st century CE, monks like Faxian and Xuanzang journeyed from China to the Indian subcontinent in search of Buddhist scriptures, leaving behind detailed chronicles that highlighted mutual respect, not mistrust. For centuries, the Himalayas were not walls of division but bridges of learning, as Nalanda University and the Silk Route opened avenues for dialogue, not discord.

However, the modern nation-state era altered the dynamic dramatically. After India's independence in 1947 and the Communist Party's consolidation of power in China in 1949, the relationship took a political turn. India was one of the first non-Communist nations to recognize the People's Republic of China, extending a hand of ideological neutrality and Asian solidarity. Prime Minister Nehru envisioned a "brotherhood" between the two post-colonial states, captured in the phrase *'Hindi-Chini Bhai Bhai'*. **The Panchsheel Agreement** of 1954, built on mutual respect for sovereignty and territorial integrity, was meant to institutionalize that vision. But idealism would soon collide with realpolitik.

The **1962 Sino-Indian War** shattered that brotherhood. Sparked by unresolved border disputes, particularly in Aksai Chin and Arunachal Pradesh, China's surprise military offensive exposed India's lack of preparedness and Beijing's strategic opportunism. It wasn't just a conflict of boundaries—it was a betrayal of trust. Despite diplomatic engagements, treaties, and Nehru's efforts to de-escalate, China pursued a path that combined sudden aggression with long-term ambiguity. While India viewed borders as negotiable through dialogue, China manipulated cartography to establish new realities by force. The war left deep scars on India's psyche and fundamentally altered its security calculus.

Since then, the boundary issue has remained a persistent thorn, despite several confidence-building measures. Agreements in **1993 (Maintenance of Peace and Tranquility along the LAC)** and **1996 (Confidence Building Measures in the Military Field)** sought to avoid another war, but never resolved the fundamental issue: the absence of a mutually agreed-upon Line of Actual Control. In the decades that followed, India sought to pursue a dual-track approach—engaging diplomatically while modernizing its defence posture. Yet, China consistently leveraged ambiguity to its advantage, often speaking of *"peaceful co-existence"* while pursuing infrastructure upgrades and strategic encroachments along the LAC.

The **2020 Galwan Valley** clash marked a turning point in post-1962 India-China military relations. It was the first instance of combat fatalities in over four decades, and it shattered the illusion that diplomacy alone could prevent escalation. Indian soldiers, despite being unarmed due to prior disengagement protocols, fought with unimaginable courage, defending their sovereign ground with bare hands. The loss of 20 Indian soldiers and an undisclosed number of Chinese casualties triggered a new wave of nationalism and scrutiny. More than bullets, it was the betrayal of trust that wounded India. How could China, a permanent member of the UN Security Council, violate long-standing agreements with such calculated aggression—while simultaneously issuing calls for "calm" at international forums?

What followed was a multi-dimensional Indian response. Militarily, India strengthened its position in Eastern Ladakh, enhanced surveillance, and fast-tracked border infrastructure. Diplomatically, it engaged in nearly a dozen rounds of Corps Commander-level talks, asserting its resolve while keeping the door open for peace. Strategically, India began recalibrating its engagement with China—not by abandoning dialogue, but by recognizing that peace must be rooted in parity, not merely protocol.

Economically, the post-Galwan era witnessed India banning over 300 Chinese apps, including TikTok, citing national security concerns. While bilateral trade still exceeds $110 billion, India is now actively reducing dependency on Chinese critical tech sectors while diversifying global supply chains through initiatives like the Quad. China may remain a top trading partner, but the trust deficit has ensured that economic ties can no longer mask political tensions.

A deeper concern lies in China's behaviour as a regional and global power. It consistently speaks of non-interference and sovereignty, yet supports Pakistan's claims on Kashmir while suppressing dissent in Hong Kong and persecuting Uighurs in Xinjiang. It criticizes Western alliances as containment strategies, while itself pursuing neo-colonial influence through the Belt and Road Initiative—including the China-Pakistan Economic Corridor, which traverses Pakistan-occupied Kashmir. How can China claim neutrality when it violates India's territorial integrity in pursuit of its own economic corridors? This hypocrisy erodes Beijing's credibility—not just with India, but with much of the global South.

China's repeated blocking of India's efforts to designate Pakistani terrorists like Masood Azhar as global threats at the UN Security Council further exposes its double standards. While it lectures the world on terrorism, it shields actors who have spilled innocent Indian blood. This isn't diplomacy—it's dangerous duplicity.

India, for its part, has shown restraint and maturity. It hasn't allowed temporary tensions to destroy long-term possibilities. It continues to engage China through platforms like **BRICS, SCO, and RIC (Russia-India-China)**, but with greater realism. Prime Minister Modi's approach emphasizes strategic autonomy, refusing to be either antagonistic or submissive. India does not seek conflict—but neither will it be coerced.

The road ahead remains complex. Both nations are nuclear powers, home to over a third of humanity. Another conflict is not an option—it would not only destabilize Asia but also send shockwaves across global markets, climate cooperation, and geopolitical balances. Yet peace cannot be founded on one-sided restraint. For genuine peace to emerge, China must walk the talk. It must honour its commitments, clarify its borders, and respect India's sovereignty—not just in words, but in action.

India's message is clear: we seek cooperation, not confrontation. But cooperation must come with clarity, not covert ambitions. Strategic trust is not built on summits and slogans—it is earned by consistency and respect. The dragon may be fierce, but even a dragon must pause and ask: *'What legacy does it want to leave? One of deception and dominance, or one of responsibility and reform?'*

In the end, both civilizations have enough wisdom from their ancient pasts to shape a new Asian century—not through competition over borders, but through collaboration across challenges. Climate change, global health, energy security, and regional stability all demand joint leadership. But that partnership must be rooted in equality, transparency, and mutual respect—not tactical manipulation disguised as diplomacy.

India is rising—but it is rising responsibly. It hopes that China, too, chooses the path of mature power—not masked expansionism. The world watches, not just what India and China do, but what they become. And the time has come to decide: Will they be rivals in suspicion or partners in shaping peace?

Modern India: Dealing with World

Modern Indian diplomacy remains firmly anchored in its rich civilizational heritage while skillfully adapting to the shifting dynamics of a complex and multipolar world. The values that once guided ancient Indian rulers, philosophers, and reformers now manifest in nuanced policies and diplomatic engagements that reflect both continuity and change. At the heart of India's foreign policy lies the principle of **strategic autonomy**—a deep-rooted commitment to safeguarding the nation's sovereign decision-making in international affairs. This principle, shaped during the Cold War era through India's leadership in the Non-Aligned Movement, remains relevant today as India navigates a world marked by great power rivalry and global interdependence. Rather than aligning blindly with any single power bloc, India maintains a balanced posture, engaging constructively with a diverse range of partners—from the United States and Russia to the European Union, Japan, and the Global South—while retaining the ability to assert its national interests independently.

Another cornerstone of Indian diplomacy is the unwavering belief in the **peaceful resolution of conflicts**. Consistent with the teachings of both Kautilya and Mahatma Gandhi, India emphasises dialogue, negotiation, and diplomacy as the preferred tools of international engagement. Whether mediating regional disputes, participating in United Nations peacekeeping missions, or hosting high-level talks, India advocates for solutions that prioritise de-escalation, justice, and mutual understanding. This approach has helped position India as a responsible and stabilising force in regions of strategic importance, including South Asia, the Indo-Pacific, and West Asia.

In tandem with these efforts, India maintains a strong commitment to **respect for international law** and the principles enshrined in the **United Nations Charter**. Indian diplomats regularly champion multilateralism and global governance frameworks that promote fairness, equity, and cooperation. From climate change negotiations and disarmament talks to trade reforms and cyber diplomacy, India seeks to shape international norms that reflect the voices of emerging economies and developing nations. Upholding a rules-based international order is not merely a strategic choice for India; it is a reflection of its civilisational belief in *dharma*—the rule of law and ethical conduct in public life.

Underlying all of these principles is the philosophical ideal of ***Vasudhaiva Kutumbakam***, an ancient Sanskrit maxim that translates to "the world is one family." This ethos continues to influence India's global engagement, inspiring a foreign policy that is inclusive, compassionate, and culturally attuned. It is seen in India's development partnerships with African and

Asian nations, humanitarian assistance during natural disasters, and cultural diplomacy that fosters mutual respect across civilisations. Initiatives like *Vaccine Maitri*, which provided COVID-19 vaccines to over 90 countries, and India's leadership during crises such as the Ukraine conflict (Operation Ganga) or earthquakes in Turkey and Nepal, are practical embodiments of this timeless principle. ***Vasudhaiva Kutumbakam***, thus, is not just a moral ideal—it is a living philosophy that guides India's diplomatic behaviour in the 21st century.

Together, these pillars—strategic autonomy, peaceful conflict resolution, adherence to international law, and the embrace of a global family—form the soul of modern Indian diplomacy. They ensure that while India evolves with the world, it does not abandon its roots.

G20

भारत 2023 INDIA

वसुधैव कुटुम्बकम्

ONE EARTH • ONE FAMILY • ONE FUTURE

Instead, it draws strength from them, offering a model of foreign policy that blends realism with values, and ambition with responsibility.

India doesn't shout to prove its presence—it makes the world turn its head with quiet power. A nation that once bore the chains of colonialism now shapes global conversations, not with arrogance but with clarity. It doesn't beg for respect—it commands it. And when pushed, it doesn't just push back—it rewrites the rules.

When the West draws lines, India redraws them with ink made of civilizational wisdom and 21st-century grit. When China flexes, India doesn't flinch—it fortifies. When Pakistan plots, India exposes. And when the world watches—India leads. That's not aggression; that's assertion. Diplomacy is our first instinct, but don't confuse calm with weakness. We give peace a chance—but we give war no second one.

India's diplomacy is not built on theatrics or showy alliances. It's crafted from trust, time, and tested friendships. From helping evacuate citizens of over 30 countries from war zones in Yemen and Ukraine, to sending vaccines to more than 100 nations during the pandemic—we lead with humanity, not hegemony. And when it comes to terror, India doesn't just condemn—it calls out names. Be it Balakot or Uri, we make it clear: cross the line, and we won't hold back. Our tolerance is high—but not infinite.

With the U.S., we partner with independence. With Russia, we engage with legacy. With the Middle East, we build bridges of energy and culture. With Africa, we act as equals, not exploiters. In the Indo-Pacific, we don't follow blocs—we lead coalitions. While others build pressure through propaganda, India builds policy through presence. You won't find us imposing, but you will find us indispensable.

And when China tries its salami slicing, India doesn't cry foul to the world—it sharpens its claws. Galwan was proof that the idea of India bleeds but never bows. While the dragon plays its ancient board game of Go, the elephant walks slowly, strategically, and when needed—tramples the board altogether.

At the UN, we speak with restraint. At BRICS, with relevance. At G20, with responsibility. And at home, we rise—building the world's fourth-largest economy, launching missions to the Moon, and lifting millions from poverty without losing our soul in the process. India doesn't chase headlines—it creates history.

So how does India deal with the world? With open palms and iron fists—depending on how we are greeted. We don't crave validation. We're not the East looking for Western approval—we are Bharat, a civilizational state in a modern avatar. We do what is best *for our* people.

International Organizations - Failures, Frustrations & The Indian Lens

Introduction: Between Ideals and Reality

International organizations were established in the aftermath of global turmoil—World Wars, colonial collapse, and Cold War divisions—with noble intentions: to foster peace, uphold justice, ensure cooperation, and protect human dignity. Institutions like the United Nations, the International Monetary Fund, the World Bank, and the World Health Organization were envisioned as the architects of a just global order. However, over the decades, their performance has often exposed deep-rooted biases, operational inefficiencies, geopolitical manipulation, and structural injustice—particularly visible in their treatment of countries like India, Pakistan, and other developing nations.

1. The United Nations Security Council (UNSC): An Unequal Table

India's Exclusion from Permanent Membership

India, with 1.4 billion people, the world's fifth-largest economy (as of 2023), a nuclear power, and a founding member of the UN, **remains excluded from the UNSC's Permanent Membership**. The current P5 (U.S.A., U.K., France, Russia, China) reflects the post-1945 power structure—**utterly outdated in the 21st century.**

Despite India contributing significantly to UN peacekeeping missions (over 250,000 Indian troops have served, the highest from any country) and being a responsible nuclear state, **its bid for a permanent seat has been stalled—mostly due to China's opposition and the lack of comprehensive reform in the UN Charter.** India's repeated demands, along with those of the G4 nations (Germany, Japan, Brazil, and India), for UNSC reform have been met with token debates but no action.

Pakistan's Abuse of UN Platforms

Pakistan has repeatedly internationalized the Kashmir issue at the UN, especially after the abrogation of Article 370 by India in 2019. Despite clear bilateral agreements like the Shimla Agreement (1972) mandating that all issues be resolved bilaterally, Pakistan has manipulated platforms like the UNHRC to portray a false narrative.

India has often had to defend its sovereignty in forums that should respect settled international treaties. The failure of UN agencies to condemn state-sponsored terrorism emanating from Pakistan, despite evidence, reflects how geopolitics often trumps truth.

Double Standards on Terrorism

UN-designated terror organizations like *Lashkar-e-Taiba* and *Jaish-e-Mohammed* have links to Pakistani soil, and their leaders roam free despite global sanctions. China has repeatedly blocked India's attempts at the UN to designate individuals like Masood Azhar under the 1267 sanctions list. This illustrates not only the abuse of veto power but also how powerful nations can shield allies at the expense of justice.

2. World Health Organization (WHO): The COVID-19 Cover-Up

The WHO's failure during the COVID-19 pandemic is a textbook case of institutional collapse under pressure from major powers.

- **Delayed Response**: The WHO was accused of delaying the declaration of COVID-19 as a Public Health Emergency of International Concern (PHEIC), despite China reporting the virus as early as December 2019.

- **Soft on China**: The WHO repeatedly echoed Chinese state positions, praising their "transparency" even when it was clear that vital information was being suppressed. This undermined global trust and delayed preparedness.
- **India's Marginalization**: Despite India's significant role in vaccine development, distribution (Vaccine Maitri), and digital innovation (CoWIN platform), the WHO did not acknowledge India's leadership role until much later. It failed to highlight how India supplied over 200 million vaccines globally while managing its own population.

India, which conducted one of the largest vaccination drives in human history, received minimal institutional support or credit compared to Western nations. The WHO's politicization during the pandemic has led to calls for reform, with India advocating for a more transparent and accountable WHO.

3. International Monetary Fund (IMF) & World Bank: Financial Injustice

The IMF and World Bank were designed to stabilize economies and aid development, but over time they have been criticized for:

Biased Lending Practices

- **Pakistan's Bailouts**: Pakistan has received over 22 International Monetary Fund (IMF) bailouts since 1958—the most for any country. Despite consistent misuse of funds, military overspending, and failure to implement reforms, the IMF has continued lending, often under pressure from allies like the U.S. or China.

- **India's Case**: India, on the other hand, has maintained economic prudence, sought fewer bailouts (last one in 1991), and still has little say in IMF policy formulation due to outdated quota systems. As of 2023, India's voting share in IMF is just 2.75%, compared to the US's 16.5%, despite being among the top five global economies.

Structural Adjustment Harms

Developing countries, especially in Africa and South Asia, have been forced into austerity measures that cripple public welfare under the IMF "*structural adjustment programs*." These conditions often lead to higher inequality, stagnated growth, and weakened institutions.

India's Reform Example Ignored

India's economic liberalization in 1991 was domestically driven, not IMF-imposed. It succeeded because of internal consensus, not external coercion. This is often overlooked when the IMF and World Bank push top-down reforms in smaller nations.

4. UN Human Rights Council (UNHRC): A Platform Misused

Ironically, countries with poor human rights records, including Pakistan, China, and Saudi Arabia, have held membership in the UNHRC. This undermines the body's credibility.

Selective Outrage

- **Kashmir vs. Xinjiang**: The UNHRC has issued multiple statements on Jammu & Kashmir but has been mostly silent or diplomatic on China's treatment of Uyghur

Muslims in Xinjiang, where at least one million people are believed to have been detained in re-education camps.

- **India's Response**: India has maintained a transparent democracy with an independent judiciary, free press, and human rights frameworks. Yet, it faces disproportionate scrutiny while authoritarian regimes go unchecked.

This selective bias reduces the UNHRC to a political stage rather than a human rights guardian.

5. International Court of Justice (ICJ) – Mixed Signals

While the ICJ has been a platform for fair hearings, it is still deeply constrained by the willingness of states to comply.

The Kulbhushan Jadhav Case

India approached the ICJ after Pakistan denied consular access to Indian national Kulbhushan Jadhav, who was arrested and sentenced to death by a military court in 2017.

- The ICJ ruled in India's favor, stating that Pakistan violated the Vienna Convention.
- However, Pakistan has since dragged its feet in implementing the judgment, refusing meaningful access or retrial.

This exposes the weakness of international law enforcement. ICJ can pass judgments, but it cannot enforce them. In politically sensitive cases, especially involving military matters, compliance is rare unless major powers intervene.

6. Climate & Trade: India as the Scapegoat?

India has often been targeted in climate forums like COP (Conference of Parties) for its coal usage and emissions, despite being one of the lowest per capita emitters.

- **Fact**: India emits 1.9 tonnes of CO_2 per capita (2022), far less than the U.S. (14.4) and China (7.6). Yet, it is frequently asked to cut emissions on par with industrialized nations.
- **Trade Barriers**: Developed countries often use environmental or labor standards as trade barriers against Indian exports, while ignoring their own histories of industrial pollution.

India's push for climate justice—that historical emitters should bear more responsibility—is often sidelined by Western narratives that shift the burden to emerging economies.

7. WHO, WTO & the Vaccine Patent Debate

India and South Africa pushed for temporary waivers on vaccine intellectual property rights at the World Trade Organization to allow developing countries to manufacture COVID-19 vaccines affordably.

- Despite global support from NGOs and developing nations, the proposal was blocked by European nations and pharma lobbies, highlighting how profits often override lives.

India, known as the *"pharmacy of the world,"* could have produced millions more vaccines had the WTO acted swiftly. The delay cost lives—especially in Africa and South Asia.

Conclusion: Reform or Redundancy?

International organizations today face a serious credibility crisis. Their actions (or inactions) have led to a **trust deficit**, especially among nations like India that are rising in stature but not getting proportional voice or respect.

India's criticisms are not against global cooperation, but against the unjust hierarchies and structural inertia that these bodies protect. A truly equitable world order cannot be built on systems that reflect the past, ignore ground realities, and serve selective interests.

As India takes on greater global responsibilities—be it G20 leadership, climate action, or humanitarian aid—it must also continue advocating for **institutional reforms** that democratize power, promote accountability, and reflect modern realities.

International organizations must evolve—or risk becoming relics of a failed global order.

In a world that hinges on collective action, international organizations were envisioned as guardians of peace, justice, development, and human dignity. Institutions like the United Nations (UN), the World Health Organization (WHO), the International Monetary Fund (IMF), and the World Bank were built on the ruins of global conflict and economic despair. Yet, as the 21st century unfolds, glaring questions remain: Have these institutions truly served humanity equitably, or have they become bureaucratic behemoths, often paralyzed by politics, partiality, and procrastination?

This chapter dissects the global failures of major international organizations, underlining how their structural limitations, geopolitical compromises, and sometimes even complicity have left millions of lives unprotected and countless crises unresolved.

1. The United Nations – Paralyzed by Power Politics

Syria: A Crisis Frozen in Time

Since the Syrian Civil War began in 2011, over 500,000 people have been killed and nearly 13 million displaced. The UN Security Council, the body mandated to maintain global peace and security, has been largely ineffective due to the **veto power of its five permanent members (P5)**. Russia, a staunch ally of the Assad regime, has **vetoed at least 17 resolutions** aimed at humanitarian access or sanctions against Damascus. This deadlock has not only prolonged the war but also damaged the UN's credibility.

Rwanda Genocide: A Shameful Silence

In 1994, over 800,000 Rwandans—mostly Tutsis—were massacred in a span of 100 days. Despite warnings from the UN's own peacekeeping force, **no robust intervention occurred**. The UN Security Council not only ignored early warnings but also **withdrew peacekeeping troops**, leaving civilians defenseless. Former UN Secretary-General Kofi Annan later called this *"one of the darkest chapters in human history."*

Yemen: The Forgotten War

In Yemen, the United Nations has repeatedly failed to broker a lasting ceasefire between the Iran-backed Houthis and the Saudi-led coalition. Even as **millions face famine**, international responses remain slow, politicized, or ineffective, revealing how humanitarian action often falls prey to geopolitical interests.

2. The WHO – Politics Over Public Health

COVID-19: Delay, Denial, and Diplomatic Fragility

The **World Health Organization's (WHO)** handling of the COVID-19 outbreak raised global concern. Despite early reports of human-to-human transmission in Wuhan, China, the **WHO delayed declaring a Public Health Emergency of International Concern (PHEIC)** until January 30, 2020. Even then, it hesitated to label COVID-19 a pandemic until March—**precious months were lost**.

Moreover, the WHO's **overreliance on Chinese state data** and reluctance to question China's early narratives led to accusations of bias and weakened trust in the institution. Independent investigations revealed that the WHO ignored warnings from whistleblowers and suppressed internal discussions due to **fear of offending member states**.

Ebola in West Africa: A Slow Burn

During the 2014 Ebola outbreak in Guinea, Liberia, and Sierra Leone, WHO was again criticized for its **delayed response**. Although cases began in December 2013, a global health emergency was declared **only in August 2014**, by which time the virus had spread uncontrollably, killing over **11,000 people**.

3. IMF and World Bank – Debt, Dependency, and Development Delusions

Debt Traps in Africa and Latin America

The **International Monetary Fund (IMF)** and **World Bank** have long been accused of imposing structural adjustment programs that often **prioritize austerity over human development**. In countries like Ghana, Argentina, and Zimbabwe, the IMF-prescribed cuts in healthcare, education, and subsidies have worsened poverty and sparked civil unrest.

In Africa, 21 countries spend **more on debt servicing than on public health**, often due to the IMF loans with conditionalities that restrict fiscal sovereignty. These institutions have created **dependency cycles**, forcing nations to take repeated loans without long-term developmental gains.

Argentina: A Revolving Door of Bailouts

Since 1958, **Argentina has received over 20 IMF bailouts**, the largest being **$57 billion in 2018**. Despite this, the country continues to suffer from inflation, recession, and debt crises. Critics argue that the IMF policies have **prioritized creditor interests** over citizens' welfare, proving ineffective in achieving sustainable economic recovery.

4. UNHRC – The Irony of Human Rights Watchdogs

The **United Nations Human Rights Council (UNHRC)**, created to uphold and protect human rights globally, has often drawn criticism for its **membership list**, which has included nations with **poor human rights records**—like Saudi Arabia, China, Venezuela, and Eritrea. Their presence **undermines the**

Council's legitimacy, turning it into a theater of selective criticism and political grandstanding.

Moreover, the Council's focus is frequently skewed. While Israel has faced more resolutions than North Korea or Myanmar, large-scale human rights abuses in countries like China (Xinjiang), Russia (Chechnya), and Iran often receive **mild or no condemnation**. This raises valid concerns about **geopolitical bias and tokenism** in global rights discourse.

5. Climate Change & COP Summits - All Talk, No Accountability

The **United Nations Framework Convention on Climate Change (UNFCCC)** has convened 28 Conferences of the Parties (COPs), yet emissions continue to rise, glaciers keep melting, and island nations inch closer to extinction. The **Paris Agreement (2015)** was historic in intent but lacked **enforceable penalties** for non-compliance.

Major polluters like the U.S., China, and the EU routinely fall short of targets, yet face no real consequences. Meanwhile, developing countries—who contribute least to climate change—bear the brunt of its effects, from rising sea levels in the Maldives to desertification in the Sahel.

The **Green Climate Fund**, promised to support poorer nations, remains **underfunded and underutilized**, illustrating how climate justice often becomes a victim of broken promises.

6. Refugee Crises – Stateless and Forgotten

Rohingya Crisis

In 2017, over 700,000 Rohingya Muslims fled Myanmar amid what the UN itself described as **"a textbook case of ethnic cleansing."** Yet, no substantive sanctions were imposed on Myanmar's military. The Security Council remained silent due to China's and Russia's veto threats, and ASEAN countries offered only token diplomatic protests.

The UNHCR (United Nations High Commissioner for Refugees) has provided relief but failed to ensure **safe repatriation**, allowing the crisis to linger for years without a durable solution.

Syrian Refugees and European Hypocrisy

While international agencies like UNHCR coordinate camps in Lebanon, Jordan, and Turkey, **European Union member states have often refused to share the burden**, erecting border fences and limiting asylum quotas. The **2015 EU-Turkey deal**, which outsourced refugee control to Ankara in exchange for funds, effectively **shifted responsibility without accountability**.

7. Israel–Palestine: Decades of Deadlock

The United Nations has passed **hundreds of resolutions** concerning the Israeli-Palestinian conflict, yet most remain unenforced. The Security Council's actions are often **blocked by the United States**, shielding Israel from punitive measures despite international concerns over settlement expansions and human rights violations.

The **failure to broker a two-state solution**, despite decades of diplomacy, reflects how international institutions are often unable to enforce peace when superpower interests are involved.

8. Afghanistan: 20 Years, Trillions Spent, No Peace

The US-led war in Afghanistan, once backed by a coalition of NATO and endorsed by the UN, ended in 2021 with the **Taliban's return to power**. After two decades, over 200,000 civilian deaths, and trillions of dollars spent, international organizations were unable to ensure either peace or development.

The **UN Assistance Mission in Afghanistan (UNAMA)** has struggled to operate under Taliban rule. Meanwhile, **Afghan women and minorities** face systemic erasure from public life, and international promises to protect them have proven hollow

From the ashes of two world wars, the modern world inherited more than just trauma; it inherited resolve. Institutions like the United Nations, the World Health Organization, the International Monetary Fund, the World Bank, and several specialized agencies were born not merely as bureaucratic centers but as moral commitments. Over the decades, they have served as anchors of peace, hope, and collaboration.

The United Nations has prevented global escalation of numerous regional conflicts and has acted as a convening platform even during the worst diplomatic deadlocks. Its peacekeeping operations, often unsung, have silently saved generations from cycles of war. The WHO, in its long journey, led humanity to one of its proudest public health victories: the eradication of smallpox. It has managed countless outbreaks, served as a voice for equitable access to health, and continues to champion the cause of universal health coverage. The IMF and the World Bank have pulled nations from the brink during financial storms, helping lay the foundation for modern economies and infrastructure. In times of crisis—whether natural, financial, or geopolitical—these institutions have risen to respond.

However, the nature of crises has evolved. The 21st century brings challenges that are no longer confined to borders: Pandemics that travel through airports, disinformation that travels through cables, and climate catastrophes that ignore sovereignty. Thus, the need is not to abandon or criticize these organizations, but to empower and evolve them with time, acknowledging that what was designed for a post-WWII world must now be remodeled for a digital, interconnected, climate-fragile globe.

For the United Nations, the next phase must be characterized by renewed inclusivity and agility. Its credibility and relevance would soar further if the Security Council became more reflective of current geopolitical realities. Including countries like India, Brazil, South Africa, Nigeria, and others not only makes structural sense due to their economic and demographic weight, but also infuses the council with the voice of the Global South, which is essential for balanced policymaking.

This expansion must also be accompanied by stronger institutional backing for peacebuilding rather than mere peacekeeping. While blue helmets guard borders, real peace requires rebuilding institutions, restoring justice, and healing trauma. A permanent peacebuilding wing with secure funding, regional expertise, and cultural sensitivity can transform how the UN is seen on the ground. Moreover, the UN must not just be a reactive body—it must be predictive. By integrating artificial intelligence, real-time satellite analytics, and regional data observatories, it can create an early warning system to detect signs of ethnic conflict, forced migration, or environmental degradation long before catastrophe strikes. Such digital evolution would position the UN as a proactive force in the 21st century.

Similarly, the World Health Organization must be praised for its tireless work during global health crises—from coordinating international responses to Ebola and COVID-19 to its constant surveillance of infectious diseases. But now, it must be equipped with tools of the future. A legally binding global pandemic treaty would be a step forward—where countries agree to share data, grant access to inspection teams, and ensure vaccine equity during future outbreaks. Instead of relying solely on temporary pledges, the WHO must have access to a permanent global health emergency fund, allowing it to respond swiftly and decisively the moment an outbreak is reported. Building regional health hubs, especially in regions like Sub-Saharan Africa and South Asia, can decentralize response capacity and reduce delays.

In the economic sphere, the International Monetary Fund (IMF) and the World Bank deserve appreciation for offering emergency packages during COVID-19 and steering economies through volatile debt cycles. Their support to fragile economies like Sri Lanka, Pakistan, Greece, and many African nations has often been the thin line between collapse and recovery. That said, they must evolve toward a more development-sensitive approach. Countries should not have to choose between fiscal discipline and investing in public health or education. Loan conditionalities must be more customized, grounded in local socioeconomic realities, and aligned with the UN Sustainable Development Goals.

Moreover, the IMF's governance structure, often based on legacy voting rights, can be rebalanced to reflect today's multipolarity. Voices of emerging economies—like India, Indonesia, Brazil, and Nigeria—must gain proportional influence in global financial rule-making. This not only ensures fairness but also deepens institutional legitimacy.

Additionally, with climate change threatening the very foundation of economies, these institutions can champion a just green transition. Establishing a Global Green Transition Fund under the World Bank that supports countries shifting to renewable energy while protecting vulnerable jobs would help bridge the development-environment gap. IMF's debt relief frameworks must become more accessible and enduring, allowing countries to pause debt service during global shocks like pandemics or disasters without risking creditworthiness.

The issue of displacement, perhaps the most heart-wrenching of global problems, demands similar reform rooted in compassion and realism. The UNHCR and IOM have done heroic work under impossible circumstances, providing food, shelter, and legal identity to millions fleeing war, persecution, or climate destruction. But refugee response must evolve beyond temporary camps and stopgap aid. The world can collectively establish a Global Compact for Equitable Refugee Sharing, where nations voluntarily opt into hosting a proportional number of refugees based on GDP, population, and landmass. This system—backed by a multilateral burden-sharing mechanism—would reduce pressures on frontline states while respecting global responsibility. Moreover, investing in digital identity platforms for refugees and migrants could enable continuity in education, employment, and banking regardless of where they move. Human mobility, in the future, should be met with data-driven dignity. Similarly, UNHCR can partner with educational and tech institutions to ensure children in camps don't lose years to displacement. A digital classroom in every camp, powered by solar energy and local volunteers, could be a game-changer in breaking the cycle of intergenerational poverty among displaced populations.

Climate governance has seen remarkable progress, especially with the Paris Agreement and the momentum from COP summits. The UNEP and the IPCC have provided invaluable scientific knowledge and guidance. But ambition now must translate to action. Nations must consider elevating climate commitments into legally binding compacts, with gradual enforcement mechanisms that respect sovereignty while ensuring accountability. Wealthier nations, historically the highest polluters, could help finance renewable transitions in developing countries, not as aid but as co-investments in a shared planet. This can be structured through the UN-backed carbon marketplace where nations that invest in afforestation, clean transport, or carbon capture get credits that can be traded. Beyond governments, the youth must be structurally empowered within climate decision-making. Creating a permanent Youth Climate Assembly within the UNFCCC that participates in negotiations and oversight would reflect the intergenerational nature of climate justice. The Loss and Damage Fund—approved at COP28—is a landmark, and its speedy operationalization with clear eligibility and disbursement protocols would turn hope into reality for climate-vulnerable nations.

On human rights, the UN Human Rights Council has made undeniable progress through its Universal Periodic Review, providing a forum for constructive dialogue rather than finger-pointing. To further enhance credibility, rotating membership could be conditioned upon certain baseline compliance with international human rights treaties, ensuring that the council reflects both diversity and moral standing. More resources must be committed to independent fact-finding missions, and partnerships with journalists, civil society, and satellite surveillance agencies can help overcome state resistance to access. The Human Rights Council, when equipped with real-time AI tools, could monitor human rights violations—whether attacks on minority communities, enforced disappearances, or digital repression—before they spiral into international crises. Human rights must move from being a post-conflict narrative to a pre-conflict preventive mechanism. That requires education. A global multilingual campaign to raise awareness of basic human rights through social media, school curriculums, and community programs can embed dignity into daily consciousness. The objective is not to interfere with national sovereignty, but to raise global standards of justice and liberty together.

In addition to institutional evolution, cooperation between organizations themselves can redefine response capacity. A Global Emergency Taskforce composed of rotating personnel from WHO, UNHCR, WFP, and UNDP could be deployed within 72 hours to coordinate multi-sectoral responses—combining food aid, medical support, shelter, and governance in disaster-hit regions. Meanwhile, establishing a UN Youth Volunteer Corps—open to citizens under 30—can create a new generation of diplomats, development workers, and peacebuilders trained in conflict resolution, humanitarian logistics, and community diplomacy. These volunteers could serve in UN missions worldwide and become long-term ambassadors of global citizenship. Transparency, the oxygen of accountability, must also be systematized. Real-time dashboards showing progress on SDGs, financial disbursements, climate targets, and human rights reviews can ensure public engagement and global scrutiny. Leveraging modern AI-enabled translation tools can make all UN communications multilingual, allowing communities from Somalia to Suriname to feel seen and heard.

At the heart of all these reforms lies a simple truth: **international institutions are not failing—they are evolving**. Their strength is not just in structure but in spirit. A spirit that believes in cooperation over conflict, justice over judgment, and inclusion over isolation. They have walked with humanity through wars, tsunamis, recessions, and pandemics. And as we enter an era marked by both immense peril and immense promise, their relevance grows stronger, not weaker. Reform is not a threat to these institutions—it is their rebirth. A global order rooted in empathy, shared responsibility, and mutual respect is not utopian. It is possible. And these institutions, when empowered, reimagined, and united, are the very bridges that can lead us there.

CHAPTER 4

Global Footprints of Indian Culture

India's millennia-old civilization has cast a vast cultural imprint across the world. From ancient philosophy and religious teachings to cuisine, art, literature, and modern entertainment, Indian cultural elements have travelled far beyond the subcontinent. This essay traces these influences chronologically – from ancient India's philosophical and religious movements, through medieval trade and empire links, to colonial-era diasporas and the post-independence global outreach. It highlights key dimensions of culture – philosophy and values, religion and spirituality, art and literature, language, fashion, cuisine – and how they found new homes or resonances abroad. The account includes specific case studies (e.g., yoga in the West, Ayurveda in Europe, Bollywood in Africa, cuisine in Southeast Asia, Indian diaspora in the Caribbean and Fiji), and examines India's post-1947 cultural diplomacy (Nehruvian initiatives, the ICCR, International Day of Yoga, diaspora outreach) and modern cultural icons (cricket, Bollywood, fashion, digital content). Where relevant, we note how ancient Indian epics (the Mahābhārata, Rāmāyaṇa) and ethical concepts (like **ahimsā** non-violence or *Vasudhaiva Kutumbakam* "the world is one family") underpin India's soft-power diplomacy. Throughout, we connect India's rich heritage to its contemporary global leadership narrative, using an authoritative yet diplomatic tone with detailed historical and cultural insight.

Ancient and Classical Foundations of Indian Culture

Philosophy and Spiritual Traditions

Ancient India gave rise to profound philosophical and spiritual systems. The Vedas and Upaniṣads (c. 1500–500 BCE) formulated concepts like *karma, dharma* and *mokṣa* that influenced later schools of thought. India's six darśanas (orthodox philosophical schools, including Vedānta, Sāṃkhya, Yoga, Nyāya, Vaiśeṣika, Mīmāṃsā) debated metaphysics and ethics, and ideas such as Advaita Vedānta's non-dualism found admirers abroad. The rise of Buddhism and Jainism (6th–5th centuries BCE) exemplifies India's spiritual innovation. Under Emperor Ashoka (c. 268–232 BCE), Buddhism received royal patronage and its missionaries took the *dhamma* across Asia: legend has it that Ashoka even sent his own son to Sri Lanka with Buddhist scriptures. In Sri Lanka, a Sinhalese king embraced Buddhism, after which the religion became integral to that island's culture. Similarly, Buddhist missionaries later carried teachings to Southeast and East Asia (China, Japan, Korea) during the early centuries CE, laying the foundations of the Mahāyāna and Theravāda traditions outside India.

Yoga, meditation, and spiritual practices originating in India also traveled widely. Although yoga's roots trace to the Vedic and Upaniṣadic era, its global rise came much later. By the 20th century, Indian *yogīs* and *gurus* (Paramahansa Yogananda, B.K.S. Iyengar, etc.) popularized yoga in Europe and America; today, the overwhelming number of yoga schools in America and Europe—and many parts of Asia—are a testimony to the popularity of India's rich cultural traditions. The UN's adoption of 21 June as International Day of Yoga (2014) - with over 170 countries supporting the resolution -

underscores yoga's role as a symbol of India's soft power and its appeal for well-being worldwide. Indeed, yoga's global spread through schools, festivals, and even university curricula abroad has enhanced India's image as a peace-loving country.

Finally, ancient Indian ethical values have had worldwide resonance. Most famously, Mahatma Gandhi's principle of *ahimsā* (non-violence) drew directly on India's Jain and Buddhist heritage. Gandhi applied *ahimsā* in the Indian freedom struggle, pioneering *satyāgraha* (nonviolent resistance) as a political strategy. It had an immense impact on India, impressed public opinion in Western countries, and influenced several 20th-century leaders such as Nelson Mandela and the American civil rights movement's Martin Luther King, Jr. In short, Indian philosophical and spiritual traditions - yoga, Buddhism, nonviolence, the concept of *vasudhaiva kuṭumbakam* ("the world is one family") - set the stage for many later cross-cultural exchanges and continue to inform India's self-image as a moral leader on the world stage.

Religion and Its Global Spread

Alongside philosophy, India's religions have had global reach. Ancient Hinduism (with its pantheon of deities and epic narratives) spread into Southeast Asia between the 1st–5th centuries CE, often blended with local beliefs. For example, kingdoms in present-day Cambodia, Java (Indonesia), Thailand, and Myanmar adopted Hindu deities and texts: Angkor Wat in Cambodia (12th century) was originally a Hindu temple dedicated to Viṣṇu, with its walls depicting scenes from the *Mahābhārata* and *Rāmāyaṇa*. Later it became a Buddhist shrine, showing syncretism of Indian faiths. Similarly, the Srivijaya and Sailendra dynasties of Sumatra and Java in the early medieval period were Buddhist and Hindu respectively, with Borobudur (8th–9th century CE) in Java being the largest Buddhist monument. India's Buddhist art and architecture (stupas, monasteries) influenced these regions, and Indian scholars translated scriptures for local rulers. Even as Buddhism later declined in India, it flourished abroad, contributing to the cultural heritage of places like Thailand, Sri Lanka, Tibet and East Asia.

Indian scriptures and epics themselves achieved global status. Sanskrit texts such as the Mahābhārata (including the Bhagavad Gītā) and the Rāmāyaṇa were translated early and became known in the Middle East and eventually Europe. For instance, Sir William Jones's 18th-century English translation of Kalidasa's *Shakuntala* from the Mahābhārata marked the first time a Sanskrit play reached the West. This work had a surprisingly large influence, profoundly affecting Herder and Goethe, and through the Schlegels, the entire Romantic movement in Europe. India's literary classics became part of Western literary culture. Scholars noted that Kalidasa represented the spirit of India just as Shakespeare represents England. Thus, Indian mythology and drama enriched global literature and intellectual history.

Art, Architecture and Cultural Symbols

Artistic motifs from India appear across Asia. Beyond Angkor Wat, Hindu temple architecture styles (such as the tiered towers or *gopurams* of South India) inspired monuments in Southeast Asia. Indianized kingdoms erected temples to Vishnu and Shiva (for example, Cambodia's Pre Rup and Indonesia's Prambanan), often staffed by Brahmin priests. Even statuary - Buddha images, Hindu god sculptures - reflect Indian iconography. The Silk Road and maritime trade routes carried artistic influences: Gandhara sculpture (Greco-Buddhist art) influenced East Asian Buddha images, while Persian and Hellenistic motifs mixed into Indian art in the northwest. In later eras, Indian miniature painting styles affected Mughal art in South Asia and, indirectly, later South Asian diaspora art.

Language, Knowledge and Learning

Indian languages and knowledge systems also left traces abroad. Sanskrit served as a scholarly lingua franca in much of Southeast Asia for over a millennium; many Thai, Khmer and Indonesian words derive from Sanskrit. Indian mathematicians and astronomers transmitted the concept of zero, the decimal numeral system, and algebra to the Arab world, and thence to Europe. Ayurveda (ancient Indian medicine) was practiced in Buddhist monasteries across Asia. India's early universities (e.g. Nalanda, Takṣaśilā) were attended by foreign students from China, Korea, Tibet, and the Middle East, spreading Buddhist and medical knowledge. In sum, India's ancient civilization projected philosophical, religious and scientific ideas that resonated far and wide.

Medieval and Early Modern Exchanges

Southeast Asian Civilizations and Hindu-Buddhist Kingdoms

From about the 1st to 15th centuries CE, robust trade and conquest linked India to Southeast Asia. Indian merchant guilds and Hindu/Buddhist preachers travelled by sea to Srivijaya (Sumatra), Khmer (Cambodia), Champa (Vietnam), Majapahit (Java) and Thai lands, often intermarrying with local elites. Indian religious ideas blended with indigenous beliefs, creating syncretic traditions. For example, early Thai texts show Buddhist monks speaking Sanskrit and familiarity with Upanishadic concepts; Thai cuisine was influenced by Indian spices and herbal medicine.

Architecture from this era vividly reflects Indian impact. Apart from Angkor Wat, consider Prambanan in Java (9th century CE), a massive Hindu temple complex dedicated to Shiva. Its reliefs depict scenes from the Rāmāyaṇa. The fusion of Indian myths with local lore was commonplace: in Thailand the Rāmāyaṇa became the Rāmakien epic, and in Indonesia shadow-puppet theatre (wayang) retells the Mahābhārata. These examples show how Indian epics became part of other cultures' heritage.

Artisans, Textiles and Cuisine via Trade

The medieval spice trade by sea and overland brought Indian culinary and material culture to Asia. Indian spices (black pepper, cardamom, cinnamon, turmeric, etc.) were already prized in the Roman Empire, but they also enriched Asian cuisines. Malaysian and Indonesian cuisines use Indian-inspired curries; Indonesian *rendang* (Minangkabau spicy beef dish) has clear Indian curry origins. Indian influence can be observed in Indonesia as early as the 4th century. Dishes like *biryani, murtabak* (stuffed flatbread), Indian-style curries and *paratha* influenced Acehnese, Minangkabau, Malay, Palembang and Javanese cuisines. Similarly, Thai royal cuisine has Sanskritic roots. In general, Indian spices and cooking techniques - wok/stir methods, curry pastes, lentils - spread throughout Southeast Asia.

Textiles and fashion also traveled: Indian cotton and silk fabrics were exported widely. The Indonesian *ikat* and Malaysian *batik* traditions were influenced by Indian pattern techniques. Even clothing styles mixed: in colonial times, many Southeast Asian royal courts used Indian-style turbans or sarongs adapted with local flair.

Language and Scholarship Exchange

This period also saw the spread of Indian languages and learning. Sanskrit was the *lingua franca* of religion and administration in many Southeast Asian courts. Indian numerals and astronomy went to the Arab world via traders, and Arabic merchants brought them to Europe. Medicine (*Ayurveda*) blended with Greek-Arabic systems in the Middle East. Indian chess (*Chaturanga*) likely evolved into Western chess through Persian intermediaries. In sum, medieval trade created a reciprocal cultural flow: while Indian culture influenced Asia, India in turn absorbed elements.

Culture Without Visa: How India Rewrote Global Soft Power

Modern Indian culture today is a formidable force not just in the realm of aesthetics or tradition but as a strategic tool of global diplomacy. The evolution from India's millennia-old civilization into a 21st-century cultural superpower is not accidental—it is deliberate, deeply institutionalized, and increasingly internationalized. Indian culture today is not passively exported—it is actively engaged in shaping global perceptions, foreign relations, and multilateral cooperation. Take for example, the International Day of Yoga, now celebrated in over 190 countries. What began as a spiritual tradition rooted in ancient Indian philosophy has become a globally adopted wellness movement, supported by the UN and recognized by global leaders, international athletes, and even armed forces as a tool for mental health, diplomacy, and cultural unity. This was not just cultural pride—it was cultural diplomacy in motion, orchestrated by Indian missions abroad, aligned with public diplomacy strategies, and reinforced by Indian embassies organizing global Yoga Day events from Times Square to the Eiffel Tower. Similarly, Indian food, once seen as niche or ethnic, is now part of the everyday culinary vocabulary in global capitals. The popularity of Indian spices, millet-based health diets, turmeric lattes, and regional cuisines has turned traditional Indian agriculture and recipes into billion-dollar global wellness, food-tech, and restaurant industries. India even used its G20 Presidency to declare 2023 as the International Year of Millets, positioning itself as a global champion of sustainable agriculture through indigenous knowledge. In essence, India's culture is no longer just being consumed—it is being adapted into foreign lifestyles, legislations, and institutional frameworks. It influences EU dietary regulations, global fashion runways, architectural design, and mental health policies. Countries now engage with Indian culture not as exotic novelty but as a diplomatic bridge—hosting Diwali receptions in parliaments, teaching Sanskrit in European universities, incorporating Indian classical dance into multicultural education, and collaborating with Indian design institutions for heritage preservation. The Indian Council for Cultural Relations (ICCR), operating under the Ministry of External Affairs, plays a key role here—facilitating cultural exchange programs, sponsoring global festivals, and forging academic-cultural partnerships. From ICCR's cultural centers in Berlin to Buenos Aires, India is asserting a global presence without coercion—through rhythm, not rhetoric.

Nowhere is the global footprint of modern Indian culture more visible than in its diaspora diplomacy and transnational narratives. With over 30 million Indians living abroad—the largest diaspora in the world—India has strategically transformed its expatriate population into soft power ambassadors. Cultural events organized by diaspora communities are now supported, co-hosted, and elevated by Indian diplomatic missions as part of "Bharat brand-building." Global temples, *Gurudwaras*, and cultural centers have become informal consulates of Indian philosophy and value systems. Indian dance schools, music academies, and language centers now span five continents and serve not only the diaspora but curious foreigners as well. India's cinematic industry—particularly through its international film festivals, subtitled releases, and regionally diverse content on global OTT platforms—has evolved from being diasporic nostalgia to a global narrative phenomenon. Indian cinema is now being studied in international film schools, its story arcs influencing screenwriting structures, and its moral dilemmas reflecting universal post-colonial themes. In sport, particularly cricket, India has effectively rebranded itself from participant to promoter, with international leagues now being broadcast in multiple languages across continents, drawing advertisers, tourism, and cross-border fandoms. The Indian Premier League has attracted global investment and even led to diplomatic engagements between nations. Moreover, India's soft power extends through digital diplomacy, where Indian creators dominate platforms with multilingual content that reflects regional diversity yet resonates universally. From village vlogs to classical dance reels, from cooking traditions to comic satire—India's online presence humanizes its diplomacy, especially in regions where formal political engagement is limited. Fashion, too, has been weaponized as soft power. Indian weaves, sustainable fabrics, and embroidery traditions are now centerpieces in Paris, Milan, and New York—not as borrowed exoticism but as respected craftsmanship. Initiatives like the *"Khadi for Nation, Khadi for Fashion"* campaign have turned domestic industry into global statements of ethical fashion. Similarly, Indian festivals have gone beyond community halls and are now celebrated in public squares, government buildings, and global landmarks—asserting visibility, acceptance, and cultural negotiation. The projection of modern Indian culture is strategic: it strengthens bilateral ties, cultivates economic partnerships through tourism and trade, and influences international public opinion during times of geopolitical tension. When India airlifts citizens or delivers vaccines during a global crisis, it isn't just offering humanitarian assistance—it is reinforcing its civilizational ethos of *Vasudhaiva Kutumbakam* (the world is one family), previously a philosophical line, now a cornerstone of foreign policy. Through its cultural footprint, India doesn't simply engage with the world—it invites the world into its story, weaving together diplomacy, diaspora, development, and devotion.

Culture as Diplomacy: India's Civilizational Strategy for Global Engagement

Modern diplomacy is no longer conducted solely through treaties, strategic alliances, or summits; it now flows through cultural symbolism, public perception, and soft power resonance—and India, with its civilizational depth and democratic voice, has successfully repositioned its culture as a foundational instrument of global diplomacy. Unlike many nations that build cultural diplomacy around recent historical events or industrial influence, India draws from a civilizational continuum of over 5,000 years, turning its philosophies, art forms, languages, festivals, cuisine, values, and spiritual traditions into powerful tools of international engagement. This is not mere heritage promotion—it is soft power diplomacy with purpose and precision. Culture, for India, is not an add-on to foreign policy; it is its ethical compass, a narrative vehicle, and a diplomatic lever. India's global presence today—be it through its diaspora networks, trade partnerships, multilateral institutions, or humanitarian missions—is amplified by cultural familiarity and admiration. Culture humanizes geopolitics. And in India's case, it universalizes it. Whether it's the surge of yoga studios from Montreal to Madrid, the sounds of Indian classical instruments being taught in conservatories in Vienna, the presence of Indian spirituality in world literature syllabi, or the widespread celebration of Diwali in non-Indian majority countries, India's culture has entered the bloodstream of global society. It is soft power turned into strategic influence. Cultural diplomacy operates through symbolism—and Indian diplomacy has mastered this subtly over decades. The recognition of the International Day of Yoga by the United Nations in 2014, co-sponsored by 177 countries, was more than a ceremonial victory; it was a signal that India's spiritual tradition could serve a global purpose in public health, mental well-being, and international harmony. Every year since, Indian embassies coordinate yoga events across the world—at UNESCO in Paris, in front of the UN headquarters in New York, along the beaches of Bali, and inside European parliaments—transforming an ancient Indian practice into an apolitical global ritual. This diffusion of Indian culture does not demand assimilation—it invites engagement. The world is not asked to become Indian, but to learn from India's cultural depth. This is diplomacy without pressure, influence without coercion.

Moreover, the Ministry of External Affairs has institutionalized cultural diplomacy through the Indian Council for Cultural Relations (ICCR), which has established over 35 cultural centers abroad, from Cairo to Tokyo, facilitating language learning, dance and music classes, art exhibitions, film festivals, and intellectual exchanges. These centers act as "mini-embassies of Indian thought," allowing foreign citizens to access Indian culture firsthand and building cross-cultural empathy even in regions where geopolitical ties may be under strain. This cultural continuity is further sustained through scholarships for foreign students, academic partnerships, chair professorships in international universities, and exchange programs that embed Indian civilizational values within global academic and artistic discourse. Culture helps establish relationships where hard diplomacy cannot. In conflict-prone regions or politically complex countries, cultural diplomacy creates neutral grounds for communication. For example, Indian music, dance, and cuisine have been used as tools of reconciliation and goodwill in South Asia, the Gulf, and parts of Africa, where formal diplomacy has faced resistance. India's public diplomacy—especially post-2000—has evolved to use culture as a conversation starter with the Global South. In Africa, India's cultural presence is deeply appreciated not just due to Bollywood or diaspora, but because of common post-colonial struggles, spiritual affinities, and cultural humility. India avoids cultural superiority, instead presenting its culture as pluralistic, inclusive, and co-creational. This makes Indian culture particularly effective in building bridges across diverse belief systems and governance models. In Southeast Asia, India's **Act East Policy** is culturally anchored. Shared heritage from the Ramayana, temple architecture, Sanskrit-origin words in local languages, and maritime trade traditions offer a historical foundation for modern strategic ties. Culture here becomes an enabler of geopolitical alignment, economic cooperation, and regional trust. The shared cultural geography with nations like Indonesia, Cambodia, Thailand, Vietnam, and Myanmar allows India to speak a language of unity amid political differences. Similarly, in West Asia, Indian festivals, food, and film are a part of everyday life—not just within the Indian diaspora but in mainstream society. This helps Indian diplomats navigate sensitive terrains with cultural trust as a buffer and bridge.

In multilateral forums like the G20, SCO, BRICS, and UN, India strategically uses cultural symbolism to assert its voice as a civilizational power. During its G20 presidency, India not only focused on economic agendas but highlighted millets—traditional Indian grains—as a symbol of sustainability and food security, earning global endorsements and policy discussions. This was more than agricultural promotion; it was civilizational storytelling repurposed for modern relevance. Similarly, India's proposal of "*One Earth, One Family, One Future*" during global climate discussions, rooted in the Sanskrit ethos of *Vasudhaiva Kutumbakam*, transformed a cultural principle into a planetary vision, embraced by countries looking for non-Western philosophical frameworks for sustainability and equity. In this way, India offers not just policy solutions, but philosophical scaffolding. Its culture becomes its policy language. This is evident in how India approaches global crises. When India led one of the largest vaccine donation drives in the world under "**Vaccine Maitri**," it did so not as a transactional donor but as a civilizational ally, echoing cultural values of care and compassion. The gesture was not couched in dominance, but in Dharma. In Latin America, Europe, and the Caribbean, such acts were not interpreted through Cold War binaries but through cultural affinity, winning public trust and diplomatic goodwill. Meanwhile, in the digital sphere, India's cultural influence is fast outpacing its physical diplomacy. Through social media, Indian cultural content—be it traditional crafts, regional festivals, folk dances, devotional songs, or historical storytelling—is going viral across continents. Platforms like YouTube, Instagram, and TikTok have become vehicles for India's cultural soft power, with millions around the world engaging with Indian content without any mediation from the state. This organic diplomacy is incredibly powerful because it bypasses politics and speaks directly to people's emotions and aesthetics. Even India's traditional knowledge systems—like Ayurveda, classical arts, meditation, and environmental ethics—are entering global curricula and shaping wellness industries. Cultural startups promoting Indian heritage in sustainable ways—from eco-tourism to organic cuisine—are forming part of India's commercial diplomacy. Thus, culture is not just moral influence—it's also economic strategy.

In global cities, Indian festivals like Holi and Diwali are no longer just diaspora events—they are hosted by universities, city governments, and even international institutions. These festivals become opportunities for Indian missions to not only celebrate tradition but also engage with lawmakers, business leaders, and media under the umbrella of cultural exchange. Cultural events help humanize India's image and facilitate informal diplomacy. At the World Economic Forum in Davos, India's pavilions often showcase handicrafts, cuisine, and cultural storytelling—blending Brand India with Civilizational India. In trade expos, India now leads with culture first, using it to differentiate its identity in an increasingly homogenized global marketplace. Even India's tourism diplomacy is culture-heavy, with the "Incredible India" campaign emphasizing heritage circuits, yoga tourism, Buddhist trails, and experiential crafts, appealing not just to leisure travelers but to cultural seekers, spiritual tourists, and knowledge pilgrims. This has diplomatic dividends—boosting foreign exchange, increasing people-to-people connections, and reinforcing India's image as an open, plural, safe society. Education diplomacy also carries a strong cultural layer. Indian classical arts, Indology, and philosophy are increasingly present in global universities, with growing demand for courses in Sanskrit, Indian ethics, South Asian literature, and comparative religion. Indian scholarships such as ICCR, Study in India, and special schemes for African, Central Asian, and ASEAN students integrate cultural exposure into academic engagement. India is thus shaping future thought leaders worldwide not through propaganda but by sharing its intellectual heritage. Furthermore, the Indian diaspora itself acts as a cultural diplomatic corps. Across North America, Europe, Africa, Southeast Asia, and the Gulf, the diaspora conducts festivals, runs schools of Indian music and dance, builds community halls, and engages in civic activism—constantly showcasing India's pluralism and warmth. The Government of India recognizes this role and institutionalizes it through events like *Pravasi Bharatiya Divas* and diaspora outreach programs, ensuring that the global Indian identity is linked to India's foreign policy objectives. The diaspora acts as both bridge and buffer, helping smooth relations during tense political climates and amplifying India's image when needed.

The future of Indian diplomacy lies in its ability to fuse power with purpose, strategy with soul. Culture enables that fusion. Unlike military strength or economic clout, culture cannot be sanctioned, blocked, or ignored—it seeps in, inspires, and stays. It opens doors before embassies do. It tells stories that statistics can't. Indian culture, being deeply non-threatening and philosophically inclusive, makes India a natural leader in a multipolar world where trust, identity, and narrative are increasingly shaping foreign policy. Culture has allowed India to lead without imposing, to influence without intervening. It builds coalitions not only of governments but of minds and hearts. In the great theatre of 21st-century diplomacy, where national image, soft power, and public perception matter more than ever, India's civilizational toolkit—its poetry, philosophy, wellness traditions, ethical frameworks, and festive joy—is not a relic of the past. It is its diplomatic script for the future.

CHAPTER 5
Power of Potential: Why Youth Matters?

Introduction: The Pulse of Tomorrow

Youth is not merely a fleeting stage of life or a statistic in population data; it represents the very pulse of tomorrow, the raw, undiluted energy that propels societies forward. Across every culture and nation, young people are the most dynamic source of hope, creativity, and transformation. They embody possibility in its purest form—an open canvas awaiting the brushstrokes of experience, knowledge, and opportunity. To speak of youth is to speak of potential—the latent power that, when nurtured, becomes the engine for societal evolution. This potential fuels innovation, revolutionizes economies, challenges outdated structures, and redefines cultures.

Yet, youth is also a fragile juncture in life's journey. Without proper guidance, education, and empowerment, this energy risks being squandered or diverted toward destructive paths. Therefore, understanding why youth matters is not simply about recognizing their numbers or youthful vigor; it is about acknowledging the profound role they play as architects of the future.

Globally, youth constitute a significant portion of the population. In many developing nations, they form the majority—a demographic dividend that can either be a catalyst for unprecedented progress or a tinderbox for social instability. Harnessing this power is one of the pivotal challenges of the 21st century. It requires more than token gestures; it demands systemic change that prioritizes youth empowerment as a strategic imperative for sustainable development, peace, and prosperity.

Historical Reflections: Youth as Catalysts of Change

History teaches us that youth have always been at the forefront of transformation. Their idealism, passion, and willingness to challenge the status quo have sparked revolutions, social reforms, and cultural renaissances across continents and centuries. From the democratic revolutions of the 18th and 19th centuries to the civil rights and independence movements of the 20th, young people have acted as the conscience and conscience-makers of societies. In the struggle for independence, youth played a pivotal role by mobilizing mass movements, organizing protests, and spreading nationalist ideas that transcended borders and ideologies. Their activism united disparate groups around common aspirations for freedom, equality, and justice. This pattern repeats itself across contexts: youth are often the first to recognize injustice, the most willing to take risks, and the most able to envision alternatives to oppressive systems. Their contributions are not limited to politics; youth have been crucial to cultural innovations, scientific breakthroughs, and social entrepreneurship. Their voices, when heard and respected, have the power to reshape entire nations and influence global directions. However, history also reveals the tragic consequences when youth potential is suppressed or ignored. Exclusion from education, employment, and political participation breeds frustration, alienation, and unrest. When denied the means to contribute positively, young people may resort to violence, extremism, or criminality as expressions of their disenfranchisement. Thus, the story of youth is not only one of hope but also one of urgent responsibility for societies to recognize and nurture this vital resource.

Education: The Keystone of Potential

Education stands as the most critical lever to unlock the potential of youth. But education is not merely about literacy or numeracy; it is about equipping young people with the tools to think critically, innovate, empathize, and navigate an increasingly complex and interconnected world. A quality education fosters curiosity, resilience, and a lifelong passion for learning, enabling youth to become active participants rather than passive observers of their societies. Around the globe, significant progress has been made in expanding access to education, but persistent challenges remain. Disparities based on gender, socioeconomic status, ethnicity, and geography continue to restrict opportunities for millions of young people. Bridging these gaps is essential to transforming youthful energy into productive power that benefits entire societies. Moreover, education systems must evolve beyond traditional frameworks and rote memorization. The demands of the 21st century require skills that nurture creativity, problem-solving, intercultural competence, digital literacy, and emotional intelligence. Integrating these competencies into curricula prepares youth to tackle complex global challenges like climate change, pandemics, technological disruption, and social inequality. Investment in education is not merely a developmental priority; it is an investment in peace and prosperity. Educated youth are more likely to participate meaningfully in democratic processes, resist extremist ideologies, and contribute to sustained economic growth. Education also empowers young women and marginalized groups, promoting social equity and cohesion. Therefore, policy frameworks must prioritize inclusive, forward-looking education models that reflect the aspirations and realities of today's youth, ensuring that no one is left behind in the march toward a better future.

Youth and Innovation: Engines of Economic Growth

Youth have an innate ability to imagine new possibilities and challenge existing paradigms, making them prime drivers of innovation and entrepreneurship worldwide. Young entrepreneurs are launching startups that disrupt traditional industries, develop cutting-edge technologies, and create social enterprises addressing critical issues ranging from environmental sustainability to public health. The digital revolution has been a game-changer, providing youth with unprecedented tools to connect, collaborate, and create on a global scale. Access to the internet, mobile technology, and online platforms has democratized knowledge and opportunity, enabling youth-led ventures to flourish even in resource-constrained environments. These innovations drive economic diversification and resilience, especially in emerging economies.

Yet, youth entrepreneurship still faces systemic barriers, including lack of access to finance, mentorship, infrastructure, and regulatory support. Overcoming these challenges requires coordinated efforts by governments, the private sector, and civil society to build ecosystems that nurture youth-led innovation. Incubators, accelerators, skill development programs, and inclusive financing mechanisms are essential components of this supportive environment.

Economic inclusion of youth goes beyond entrepreneurship alone; it encompasses employment policies that recognize the unique challenges young workers face, such as skills mismatches, job insecurity, and informal labor. Unlocking the full economic potential of youth can create a virtuous cycle by reducing poverty, fostering social stability, expanding markets, and laying the foundation for long-term growth.

Civic Engagement and Governance: Shaping Societies

Youth engagement in civic and political life is fundamental to building inclusive, accountable, and responsive societies. Young people bring fresh perspectives, boundless energy, and a commitment to justice that can revitalize democratic processes and institutions. Their participation in policymaking, electoral politics, advocacy, and grassroots movements strengthens the social fabric and promotes equity.

Around the world, youth-led movements have championed causes from environmental protection to human rights, demonstrating that young people are not only beneficiaries of policies but also critical stakeholders in shaping them. Their activism challenges complacency, holds leaders accountable, and introduces innovative solutions to entrenched problems.

However, structural barriers often limit youth participation in governance and decision-making. Age-based restrictions, limited political education, and exclusion from leadership spaces undermine their ability to contribute meaningfully. Overcoming these obstacles requires deliberate strategies such as lowering age limits for public office, integrating civic education into curricula, and creating platforms for youth consultation and leadership development. Investing in youth governance capacity is not just about inclusion; it is about securing the future. Societies that empower youth today lay the groundwork for sustainable development, peace, and social justice tomorrow.

The Role of Youth in Building Peace and Global Understanding

Youth hold a unique position in shaping peace and harmony in their societies and the world. Their energy, openness, and creativity make them powerful agents of change who can help **build bridges instead of walls**. When young people come together across cultures and borders, they create bonds of understanding that cut through the fear and mistrust often caused by ignorance. These connections are essential in today's interconnected world where conflicts can arise quickly but peace requires patience, empathy, and dialogue.

Young people have repeatedly shown that they can inspire positive movements for peace—from grassroots campaigns promoting nonviolence to global initiatives advocating for justice and human rights. Their voices are often the loudest calls for fairness, equality, and respect for all, reminding older generations of the power of hope and renewal. In many parts of the world, **youth-led peace organizations** work tirelessly to bring warring communities together, organize dialogues, and promote reconciliation. These efforts may seem small in the shadow of large-scale conflicts, but history shows that lasting peace often begins with these personal and local acts of courage and understanding.

By engaging youth in peacebuilding, societies invest not only in preventing violence today but also in nurturing leaders who will carry the torch of harmony into the future. When young people learn the values of respect, justice, and cooperation early on, they become lifelong advocates for peace who influence governments and global institutions. Peace is not just the absence of war but the presence of justice and fairness, and youth hold the key to creating these conditions. Encouraging **cross-cultural exchanges**, **peace education**, and **inclusive dialogues** are practical ways to empower youth as peacebuilders. Their potential to change the world is greatest when they feel heard, valued, and included in decisions that shape their lives and futures.

Youth and Technology: Connecting the World

The digital age has unlocked a new frontier for youth empowerment, allowing young people to connect, create, and lead like never before. Social media, online learning platforms, and digital tools provide youth with the means to share ideas, mobilize communities, and access information at a global scale. This unprecedented access to knowledge and networks has helped youth take active roles in social change, environmental activism, and political movements. They are using technology to amplify their voices and hold leaders accountable in ways that were impossible a generation ago.

However, digital technology also comes with challenges. The spread of misinformation, online hate speech, and cyberbullying threatens the positive potential of these platforms. It is essential to equip youth with digital literacy skills—helping them discern facts from falsehoods, communicate respectfully, and use technology responsibly. By doing so, we ensure that technology remains a tool for empowerment rather than division. Governments, schools, and communities must work together to create safe digital spaces where young people can thrive and contribute positively.

The power of youth in the digital world is transforming global communication and collaboration. From organizing global climate strikes to launching crowdfunding campaigns for social causes, youth show that technology can be a force for good when combined with passion and purpose. Their ability to connect beyond borders creates a new kind of global citizenship—one rooted in shared humanity rather than nationality or ethnicity. This digital connectedness can foster empathy and cooperation, key ingredients for building a more peaceful and just world.

Youth in Climate Action: Protectors of the Planet

Few issues illustrate the urgency and potential of youth like the fight against climate change. Young people across the globe have taken center stage in demanding action to protect the planet for current and future generations. Their passion and determination have sparked a global awakening to the realities of environmental crisis and the need for sustainable solutions. **Youth-led climate strikes, advocacy campaigns, and innovative environmental projects have forced governments and corporations to take notice and act.**

What makes youth such powerful climate activists is their stake in the future. Unlike previous generations, young people will live longer with the consequences of environmental degradation, making their voices critical in shaping policies that affect the planet's health. Their fresh ideas, willingness to challenge old ways, and ability to mobilize peers and communities make them invaluable allies in the fight against climate change.

Supporting youth in climate action means providing education, resources, and platforms for their ideas to flourish. It means recognizing their right to participate in environmental decision-making and ensuring intergenerational dialogue where young and old work side by side. This collaboration between generations is vital because solving climate change requires the wisdom of experience and the courage of youth combined. The **planet's future** depends on how well we listen to and empower young people today.

Youth are often called the **world's greatest resource** — not just because of their energy, but because of their unparalleled potential to change the course of history. This potential manifests not in abstract ideas but through real-world actions, innovations, and leadership that have reshaped nations and global movements. To truly grasp why youth matter, one must look closely at their role in shaping peace, development, and diplomacy through concrete examples and data-driven insights.

Youth as Innovators: Catalysts of Change and Economic Powerhouses

Youth-led innovation is a driving force behind some of the most transformative economic and social changes worldwide. According to a 2023 UNESCO report, young entrepreneurs (aged 15-29) account for nearly 40% of startups globally, many focusing on technology solutions that address urgent issues such as climate change, healthcare, and education. For instance, young innovators in sub-Saharan Africa have created mobile platforms that provide remote health consultations, overcoming infrastructure challenges and improving access to care for millions.

In India, over 65% of the population is under the age of 35, and the government's "**Startup India**" initiative has fueled a youth-led startup ecosystem with over 90,000 recognized startups as of 2024. Many of these are technology-driven enterprises that generate employment and contribute to economic resilience. The youth's entrepreneurial spirit, supported by education and government policies, translates into broader social stability, which is crucial for peace. Economic opportunities reduce the allure of violence and extremism by offer

Rwanda's post-genocide recovery exemplifies how empowering youth can fuel peacebuilding. After the 1994 genocide that claimed nearly a million lives, Rwanda invested heavily in youth education and entrepreneurship. The government launched initiatives such as the "**Youth Connect**" platform, connecting young people to business resources and civic engagement programs. This approach contributed to transforming a fractured society into one focused on unity and development. Data shows that Rwanda's youth unemployment rate dropped from over 40% in 2000 to under 20% by 2022, correlating with increased social stability and reduced ethnic tensions. Quality education is directly linked to peace and stability. The World Bank estimates that every additional year of schooling can increase a country's GDP per capita by 10%. More importantly, education reduces the risk of conflict. A 2019 study by the Peace Research Institute Oslo (PRIO) found that countries with higher youth literacy rates are 35% less likely to experience civil wars or internal conflicts.

Peace education, in particular, plays a vital role in shaping young minds to resolve disputes nonviolently. For example, in Colombia, decades of conflict led to peacebuilding programs in schools focusing on dialogue, trauma healing, and reconciliation. UNESCO's report on Colombia's peace education highlights that youth participants report a 40% greater willingness to engage in community peace initiatives compared to non-participants. This shows that targeted education programs can directly influence youth behavior toward peace. The **Arab Spring** (2010-2012) offers a complex lesson on youth's dual power to inspire change and the risks when peaceful demands turn violent. Tunisian youth led protests demanding democracy and social justice, which successfully ended decades of authoritarian rule. However, the aftermath exposed challenges as economic struggles and political instability followed. This underscores that youth potential requires not only political freedom but also economic inclusion and stable institutions to translate activism into lasting peace.

Youth diplomacy is becoming institutionalized worldwide. The United Nations' Youth Delegate program, active in over 120 countries, empowers young people to participate in global decision-making on issues like climate action, human rights, and peacekeeping. The 2015 Paris Agreement on climate change saw active involvement from youth coalitions whose advocacy influenced the inclusion of ambitious emission targets.

In 2018, the UN Security Council adopted Resolution 2419, emphasizing the role of youth in peace and security efforts.

Youth-led organizations such as the Global Youth Coalition for Peace (GYCP) have facilitated dialogues in conflict zones including Myanmar and Syria, mediating between communities to reduce violence. Their unique position—trusted by peers and flexible in approach—makes youth indispensable peacebuilders on the ground.

According to the United Nations Development Programme (UNDP), peace processes involving youth leaders are **64% more likely** to result in sustainable agreements. Yet, youth are often excluded from formal peace negotiations, highlighting a gap between policy recognition and practice. Bridging this gap can increase the legitimacy and durability of peace accords.

In many post-conflict societies, young people have taken on the role of healing divisions. For instance, in Bosnia and Herzegovina, youth-led organizations have conducted intercultural dialogues to overcome ethnic distrust that fueled the 1990s war. The NGO "**Youth Connect**" organized exchange programs and storytelling workshops that allowed young Serbs, Croats, and Bosniaks to share their experiences and develop empathy.

Psychological studies reveal that youth participation in such reconciliation efforts improves mental health outcomes and reduces the likelihood of joining violent groups. UNICEF data from conflict zones like South Sudan shows that youth involved in peacebuilding report lower levels of trauma and higher community cohesion.

Sports and arts serve as universal languages through which youth engage in cultural diplomacy, breaking down barriers between divided communities. The "Football for Peace" initiative in Northern Ireland and Israel-Palestine has used youth football tournaments to foster dialogue and trust among young people from conflicting groups, reducing community violence by up to **25% during tournament periods**, according to independent evaluations.

Music and art festivals, such as the "**Youth Arts for Peace**" programs in the Balkans, have brought together youth from different ethnic backgrounds to create collaborative works, humanizing "the other" and fostering mutual respect. These initiatives demonstrate that cultural diplomacy led by youth builds social capital essential for peace.

Youth are the heartbeat of tomorrow's world — not just in numbers but in energy, vision, and the ability to reshape societies. In a rapidly changing global landscape, young people are emerging as powerful agents of diplomacy and peacebuilding. Their involvement isn't simply about handing them the baton; it's about equipping them with tools, spaces, and respect to actively shape global decisions today.

The Rising Role of Youth in Diplomacy: More than Observers, They Are Players

Historically, diplomacy has been seen as the domain of seasoned statesmen, diplomats, and policymakers. However, the 21st century is witnessing a seismic shift. Young people are no longer passive observers of international relations; they are active participants. Their voices are critical in discussions on climate change, human rights, sustainable development, and conflict resolution. Why? Because many of the issues at the heart of diplomacy will define their futures.

But how do youth gain these skills and platforms to influence diplomacy? This is where educational and experiential programs like Model United Nations (MUN) and youth parliaments become vital.

Model United Nations (MUN): The Classroom for Global Diplomacy

MUN conferences simulate the workings of the United Nations, giving students and young adults a taste of real-world diplomacy. Delegates represent countries, debate pressing global issues, negotiate resolutions, and collaborate with peers worldwide. It is more than a classroom exercise; it's a microcosm of international politics.

The appeal of MUN lies in its hands-on nature. Participants learn to:

- Research global issues deeply,
- Understand different countries' perspectives,
- Practice public speaking and negotiation,
- Build empathy and cultural awareness,
- Collaborate to find peaceful solutions.

These skills are precisely those needed in real diplomacy. MUN has expanded globally, with thousands of conferences held each year across continents. From urban centers in the United States and Europe to remote towns in Asia and Africa, young people are stepping into diplomatic roles early. In fact, several notable diplomats and international leaders credit MUN as their first step into global affairs. A survey conducted by the *International Journal of Youth Studies* in 2018 revealed that more than 75% of MUN participants developed a stronger interest in global affairs and diplomacy, and many pursued related careers. The value of this platform goes beyond skill-building; it inspires a global mindset and sense of responsibility. Parallel to MUN, youth parliaments function as real or simulated legislative assemblies where young people debate policy, engage with leaders, and influence decision-making. Countries like Canada, the UK, Australia, and India have formalized youth parliaments as institutional spaces to listen to young citizens.

For example, India's National Youth Parliament, launched by the government, engages youth in discussions on governance and social issues. This platform encourages young voices to be heard by policymakers, fostering participatory democracy from an early age.

These forums are not symbolic; they affect real policy. Recommendations from youth parliaments have shaped national education policies, environmental laws, and social welfare programs. This inclusion helps bridge the gap between youth aspirations and governmental action, ensuring diplomacy and policy are truly intergenerational. **India stands as a vibrant example of how youth engagement is transforming diplomacy. With over 600 million people under 25, India's demographic dividend represents both a challenge and an opportunity for diplomacy.**

MUN participation in India has surged in the last decade, with numerous national and international conferences attracting thousands of delegates annually. Young Indians trained in these forums have gone on to enter the Indian Foreign Service, international NGOs, think tanks, and multilateral organizations. This grassroots diplomatic training is creating a new generation of leaders equipped to represent India on the global stage.

In addition to MUN, India's Ministry of External Affairs has implemented programs like '**Youth Connect**,' designed to foster youth diplomacy. These initiatives organize international youth exchanges, seminars, and workshops aimed at deepening cross-cultural understanding. The Indian government recognizes that empowering youth diplomatically is essential to maintaining India's growing global influence.

Youth Diplomacy in Peacebuilding: Real Impact Beyond Talks

Youth diplomacy is not just about formal negotiations; it is a powerful force in peacebuilding on the ground. Across the world, young people have been instrumental in mediating conflicts, promoting reconciliation, and rebuilding communities torn by violence.

Colombia's decades-long civil war ended in 2016 with a historic peace agreement between the government and FARC rebels. While high-level negotiations received global attention, youth organizations played a crucial, often overlooked, role in consolidating peace.

Young Colombians led grassroots initiatives to promote reconciliation, challenge violent narratives, and educate communities about peace. They used art, music, and social media to foster healing, emphasizing that peace is not just a political deal but a social transformation.

Their efforts reduced local tensions, encouraged former combatants to reintegrate peacefully, and mobilized support for democratic processes. The Colombian government publicly acknowledged that youth-led programs were vital in preventing the relapse of conflict.

Digital Youth Diplomacy: The New Frontier

Today, diplomacy transcends conference rooms and state visits. Social media and digital technology have become powerful tools in shaping international relations. Young people, who are digital natives, are at the forefront of this transformation.

Youth activists and diplomats use platforms like Twitter, Instagram, and TikTok to:

- Raise awareness on issues like climate change, human rights, and social justice,
- Mobilize international support for causes,
- Hold governments accountable,
- Create virtual dialogues that cross borders instantly.

The United Nations recognizes this shift and has launched digital initiatives to include youth voices online. The UN's Youth 2030 strategy emphasizes the importance of digital participation in global policymaking, encouraging youth-led innovation to solve complex challenges.

In recent years, the UN has increasingly invited youth delegates to participate in General Assembly debates and high-level meetings. These young representatives bring fresh perspectives and emphasize the urgency of including youth in decision-making processes.

For example, at the 2019 UN Youth Climate Summit, young delegates delivered passionate speeches demanding immediate action on climate change. Their presence signaled a paradigm shift – youth are no longer waiting on the sidelines; they are leading global conversations.

This inclusion is vital for diplomacy's future. Young voices challenge established norms, bring innovation, and demand accountability. They remind world leaders that sustainable solutions require intergenerational cooperation.

Why Youth in Diplomacy Matters: The Data Speaks

- **Demographics:** Nearly half of the world's population is under 30. Ignoring youth means ignoring the largest voting and labor bloc.
- **Global Challenges:** Issues like climate change, technological disruption, and geopolitical instability disproportionately affect youth, so their input is critical.
- **Innovation:** Youth bring fresh ideas and are more open to digital diplomacy and non-traditional peacebuilding methods.
- **Peacebuilding:** According to UN data, countries with higher youth participation in peace processes show more durable peace.
- **Economic Impact:** The World Bank estimates that investing in youth skills and employment can add trillions to global GDP.

Conclusion: Youth as the Architects of Peaceful Diplomacy

The future of global diplomacy lies in embracing youth as partners, not merely beneficiaries. Young people bring energy, creativity, and a deep commitment to a peaceful and just world. Platforms like MUN and youth parliaments are essential training grounds, while youth-led peacebuilding and digital diplomacy prove their real-world impact.

In the unfolding story of international relations, youth are not just characters; they are authors. By investing in their potential, the world can build a diplomacy that is inclusive, innovative, and anchored in peace.

Ultimately, empowering youth in diplomacy means creating accessible opportunities, building relevant skills, and valuing their contributions within national and international institutions. By integrating youth perspectives into policymaking, fostering educational platforms like MUN and youth parliaments, and supporting youth-led peace initiatives, the global community ensures that diplomacy evolves to meet the demands of the future. In this transformation, young people become not only inheritors of the world but architects of a more peaceful, just, and cooperative global order.

CHAPTER 6

Chanakya 2050

Introduction: A Vision Rooted in Legacy, A Future Forged in Resolve

India—known through the ages as *Bharat*, the cradle of civilization, the heartland of spiritual thought, and the birthplace of some of the greatest minds in philosophy, mathematics, and statecraft—stands today on the brink of a new chapter. With over a billion dreams alive in every village and city, Bharat is poised to reclaim its place as a guiding force in the global arena. This chapter, titled **"Chanakya 2050"**, pays homage to the ancient Indian strategist and philosopher Chanakya, while imagining the trajectory of India over the next three decades. It maps the country's aspirations, its probable advancements, and the conscious cultivation of a new era rooted in wisdom, vision, diplomacy, and self-reliance. As the world increasingly looks eastward, India's rise is not just a geopolitical event—it is a philosophical return, a civilizational resurgence, a renaissance long overdue.

The term **"Chanakya 2050"** symbolizes a new doctrine—merging ethical governance, economic acumen, cultural revival, and strategic diplomacy. It envisions a Bharat that leads with purpose, powered by innovation but guided by dharma (righteousness). The age of India as a reactive state must now give way to one where India becomes a proactive shaper of global norms—through technology, culture, humanitarian leadership, green energy, space diplomacy, and youth-driven democratic excellence. But to do so, India must first learn from the world—and from itself.

India's transformation will be underpinned by five critical pillars: technological sovereignty, ethical governance, educational overhaul, strategic diplomacy, and civilizational revival. These are not isolated silos but interdependent trajectories that must move in synchrony to actualize the Chanakyan vision.

By 2050, India is expected to be among the top three economies in the world. The backbone of this rise will be **technological sovereignty**—ownership over data, hardware, AI algorithms, and quantum computing. India's Aadhaar model already showcases a scalable identity infrastructure, while initiatives like UPI have revolutionized digital payments globally. The next frontier is owning the architecture—semiconductors, green chips, indigenous operating systems, and home-grown social platforms. Through schemes like **Digital India, Bharat Net**, and **PM-WANI**, the government has laid the foundation for equitable digital growth.

But **Chanakya 2050** goes further. It calls for a **Digital Dharma**—a commitment to ethical use of data and AI, respect for digital privacy, and upholding human dignity in cyber governance. In a world threatened by surveillance states and digital monopolies, Bharat's values can offer a new ethical tech standard to the world.

Education in Bharat has historically been a sacred tool—not merely to produce workers, but to create thinkers and leaders. The **New Education Policy (NEP 2020)** is a foundational shift, emphasizing critical thinking, local language instruction, and global competitiveness. But to manifest **Chanakya 2050**, India must initiate an **Educational Renaissance**—blending Vedic wisdom with cutting-edge STEM curriculum.

Imagine a system where students learn coding alongside Sanskrit logic, environmental science alongside Ayurveda, and international law alongside *Arthashastra*. Modern-day *gurukuls* with digital integration can decentralize education and personalize learning. Vocational training, global exposure, and ethical pedagogy must become core to Bharat's educational revolution. This is where India will outpace others—not in merely teaching subjects, but in **teaching character**.

Chanakya advocated for a ruler who was self-disciplined, efficient, and just. Bharat's governance in 2050 must reflect **Ram Rajya with Digital Precision**. With blockchain-based transparent governance, AI-assisted decision-making, citizen scorecards, and real-time accountability mechanisms, governance will not be limited to elections every five years. It will be a **daily feedback loop between state and citizen**.

Corruption must become not only rare but impossible through technological checks. Every citizen must have access to justice, healthcare, and safety with dignity. The model of **Antyodaya** (upliftment of the last person) must be more than rhetoric—it must be the real test of statecraft.

India's future diplomacy cannot simply react to global shifts—it must **create global shifts**. **Chanakya 2050** imagines India becoming a **moral anchor in turbulent geopolitics**—championing peace negotiations, climate diplomacy, vaccine equity, AI ethics, and South-South cooperation. From QUAD to BRICS, from G20 presidency to UN reforms—India must be a constructive disruptor.

But Bharat's soft power will be its true diplomatic currency—yoga, Ayurveda, cinema, cuisine, literature, and most of all, its ancient ethos of *Vasudhaiva Kutumbakam* (the world is one family). Indian embassies should become cultural hubs. Indian students, artists, and startups must become roving ambassadors. Cultural diplomacy must move from PR tokenism to strategic statecraft.

Bharat's future lies in its past—not in regression, but in rediscovery. The philosophies of **Chanakya, Buddha, Mahavira, Kabir, Nanak**, and **Ambedkar** must animate our future. Monuments must be restored not just in stone, but in spirit. The soul of Bharat—its tolerance, pluralism, and inner inquiry—must become its USP globally.

The narrative of Bharat must shift from one of survival to one of **symphony**—a symphony of cultures, castes, creeds, and creativity. This is not about jingoism but about **civilizational confidence**. Bharat must stop apologizing for its past and instead illuminate the path forward with it.

I believe the heart of Bharat's journey toward 2050 beats strongest in its youth. With more than half of India's population under the age of 30, the demographic dividend isn't just a statistic—it is the compass guiding our future. What excites me most is not just the number of young Indians, but their courage to question, to innovate, to dream wildly yet work diligently. Their activism, creativity, and sense of global belonging mark the beginning of a new Indian diplomacy—one driven not just by leaders in suits, but by students in Model United Nations, by young parliamentarians, by coders, poets, filmmakers, environmentalists, and grassroots changemakers.

Youth today are shaping the very vocabulary of diplomacy. Through platforms like Youth Parliaments, MUNs, startup expos, and climate marches, they are speaking directly to the world. I think these platforms are no longer extracurriculars; they are training grounds for real leadership. I have seen how an MUN conference in a small town can birth a diplomat; how a school debate on global hunger can push someone to become a UN field officer. These are no longer dreams; they are evolving realities.

In fact, when we study nations that have turned potential into power—South Korea with its tech boom, Israel with its innovation ecosystem, or the UAE with its futuristic cityscapes—we realize a common pattern: they invested in youth with a vision. And I believe Bharat can go even further. What sets Indian youth apart is their grounding in ancient wisdom and their comfort in global modernity. They chant shlokas and code in Python. They celebrate Holi and lead UN SDG campaigns. They are the bridge Bharat needs.

The roadmap to **Chanakya 2050** must now be reimagined with youth at the center. We need national youth missions that don't just train bureaucrats but prepare global diplomats, climate warriors, and digital statesmen. We need internships in embassies, fellowships in rural governance, student exchanges with Africa, Latin America, and ASEAN. Every youth must carry a passport not just for travel, but for purpose.

Our youth must become storytellers of Bharat—articulating its struggles, its solutions, and its soul to the world. Because only when the world sees Bharat through our eyes, can we truly shape our narrative. In 2050, it won't be enough for India to be known; it must be understood. And I think it is our youth who will make that happen.

If Chanakya were to return in 2050—not as a relic from the past, but as a visionary architect for the future—what would his roadmap for Bharat look like? Would he recognize the nation that once bore the spirit of *Takshashila* and *Kautilyan* statecraft? Would he marvel at our advancements or raise a brow at our lost sense of purpose? This is not a rhetorical fantasy but a philosophical necessity. To imagine a golden Bharat, we must reincarnate not just his policies, but his mindset—adapted, not adopted.

Chanakya 2050 is not about a man. It is about a method. A method rooted in clarity, courage, competence, and above all, *Chintan* (critical contemplation). It is a manifesto not merely of governance, but of civilizational awakening—a clarion call to reclaim Bharat's place as Vishwa Guru (world teacher), not through conquest, but through conduct.

Chanakya's *Arthashastra* laid down economic policy not as a standalone ambition, but as a tool for national security, societal stability, and spiritual balance. In 2050, Bharat must redefine *arthik vikas* (economic development) beyond GDP. Prosperity must be measured by sustainability, decentralization, and shared dignity.

This means **green economy zones**, **climate-smart agriculture**, and **indigenous manufacturing chains** that serve both the environment and employment. Bharat must no longer be a factory for the world, but a **laboratory of frugal innovation**. Just as the Mars mission proved excellence need not be expensive, India's villages must now prove that abundance need not be urban.

A Chanakyan Bharat would also ensure *arthik samriddhi* (economic equity). Social schemes must evolve into social platforms—interoperable welfare systems that provide universal basic needs with technological precision. Poverty alleviation must transition from aid to **architecting permanent capability**. A prosperous Bharat cannot be built on the backbone of the underpaid and the underfed.

If Chanakya's core teaching to Chandragupta was that a state must prioritize *rajaniti* grounded in *dharma,* then today's political system must cleanse itself of the drama that often overshadows duty. By 2050, India's democracy must evolve from electoral compulsions to **governance clarity**. We need **citizen charters with constitutional enforceability**, **public audits of MPs' performance**, and a **reward-penalty ecosystem** for political accountability.

Imagine a Lok Sabha that spends more time on laws than on slogans. Imagine regional leaders becoming diplomats of local heritage. Imagine political parties judged not just by manifestos but by measurable delivery. That is the Chanakyan ethic of meritocratic statecraft—**Niti (policy) over Nautanki (theatrics)**.

Chanakya famously said, "*The king who sees danger even in times of peace will always be victorious.*" This ethos must guide Bharat's national security. By 2050, threats will no longer come from just tanks and terror, but from **data theft, climate wars, AI militarization, and cognitive propaganda**. Bharat must rise as a **Neeti Yoddha (strategic warrior)**—combining physical, digital, economic, and psychological resilience.

A Chanakyan security doctrine would call for:

- **Space Defence Command** integrated with ISRO and private startups.
- **Cyber Raksha Kavach**—a nationwide shield against data colonialism.

- **Water & Food Security Forces** to tackle climate-linked conflicts.
- **Intelligence Sans Borders**—collaborative networks across friendly nations for pre-emptive counter-terrorism and intelligence

The goal is not militarization but **moral deterrence**—an India that does not need to raise its voice because its presence is already felt.

Chanakya knew that *Shakti* (power) without *Sanskriti* (culture) is blind. Bharat's cultural wealth—from its linguistic mosaic to its spiritual pluralism—is not ornamental. It is **diplomatic gold**. In 2050, India's embassies must function not merely as political offices, but as **civilizational outposts**.

Every Indian classical art form is an untapped geopolitical asset. Every festival, from Diwali to Onam, must become **soft power events** abroad. Sanskrit must be taught in foreign universities, not as nostalgia, but as a tool for AI logic and computational linguistics. India's cultural exports—from Ayurveda and yoga to philosophy and cinema—must be accompanied by **academic rigour, copyright protections, and strategic marketing**.

Cultural intelligence also means embracing diversity within. Bharat must learn to celebrate Dalit literature as much as Vedic hymns, tribal artistry alongside Mughal miniatures. Because only when Bharat fully owns its **composite cultural identity**, can it project an **authentic global image**.

Chanakya often reminded that a king without the people's support is like a cloud without rain. In 2050, the state must stop treating citizens as mere voters or beneficiaries. Instead, they must be seen as **co-authors of national destiny**. This means

participatory democracy, **policy crowdsourcing**, and **open-data governance**.

Digital infrastructure must serve as a **people's platform**—where feedback loops shape ministries, where every Indian can trace how their taxes are used, where grievance redressal is not a favor but a right. Chanakya 2050 envisions a **responsive and responsible state** that empowers local governance with national alignment.

Youth Parliaments, citizen juries, blockchain-backed voting, and digital inclusion of senior citizens and rural voices—these are not utopias. These are necessities. In a country as complex as Bharat, only **distributed empowerment** can lead to **concentrated progress**.

Chanakya 2050 is not a prediction. It is a provocation—a provocation to think bolder, act wiser, and dream longer. It is about recapturing the soul of Bharat while crafting the skeleton of a 21st-century superpower. And yet, it warns us: true greatness lies not in GDP figures or nuclear arsenals, but in the **values we export**, the **dignity we uphold**, and the **peace we propagate**.

In this vision, Bharat is:

Not a power that dominates, but one that **leads with light**.

Not a nation that conforms, but one that **redefines**.

Not a relic of the past, but a **blueprint for the future**.

Chanakya 2050 is a doctrine for the **mindful rise of a nation**—anchored in the **ancient**, elevated by the **modern**, and propelled by a **moral compass**. Because the world doesn't just need another superpower.

It needs **a guiding power**.

And that, Bharat can be.

India—known since antiquity as *Bharat*—has long stood as a beacon of civilization, a land where philosophy met mathematics, where spiritual thought shaped statecraft, and where timeless wisdom guided temporal power. From the banks of the Saraswati to the summits of Nalanda, Bharat has not merely survived history—it has shaped it. Today, as the 21st century unfolds amidst rising multipolar tensions and shifting civilizational arcs, Bharat stands poised on the threshold of a transformative epoch. This chapter—**Chanakya 2050**—does not merely glance forward; it gazes inward and then outward, tracing India's potential resurgence through the lens of one of its sharpest minds, Chanakya, the strategist, economist, and philosopher whose principles still echo in the corridors of diplomacy and power.

The vision of **Chanakya 2050** is not a dream painted in idealism but a doctrine anchored in historical memory and futuristic ambition. It reimagines Bharat not as a follower in the global order but as a shaper of it—a nation that wields technology with ethics, diplomacy with dignity, and progress with purpose. This vision combines the intellectual resilience of ancient universities, the spiritual harmony of dharmic philosophy, and the precision of digital governance. The idea is not to recreate a past glory, but to use that very heritage to mold a new, indigenous model of growth—where **GDP meets Gita**, where innovation is inseparable from introspection, and where sovereignty is both technological and spiritual. Chanakya 2050 envisions Bharat not just as a geographical entity, but as a civilizational force.

As the world increasingly looks eastward for balance, it is not enough for Bharat to rise economically—it must rise consciously. This future calls for a transition from reaction to leadership, from survival to strategy. It's a call for Bharat to emerge as a **Vishwa Guru**—not through conquest, but through **compassionate statecraft, digital dharma, ecological stewardship**, and youth-led global engagement. Chanakya 2050 is not a policy paper; it is a **civilizational manifesto**. It seeks to align Bharat's ancient spirit with modern aspirations, blending the timeless with the transformative. This isn't a prophecy—it's a **pledge**, a *Sankalp* to shape a Bharat that doesn't just navigate the future, but **defines it**.

Imagine a land where the air carries not pollution but chants of unity, where rivers flow pure and revered, and forests echo with the songs of biodiversity. Picture a Bharat where technology coexists with spirituality, where AI respects *ahimsa*, and robots follow the rhythm of *raga*. This is not science fiction—this is Bharat as **Swarga**, a utopia that is not escapist but earned, not imagined but implemented through wisdom, sacrifice, and vision.

In this Bharat, no child sleeps hungry, no woman walks in fear, no farmer dies in despair. Every home is powered by clean energy, every village is digitally connected, and every voice—regardless of caste, creed, gender, or geography—is heard. Bharat becomes the world's humanitarian capital, offering not just aid, but **ideas**; not just shelter, but **spiritual solace**. Our universities become beacons of knowledge, our temples hubs of interfaith dialogue, and our streets the theatres of innovation.

The economy blossoms not in greed, but in **green**. Skyscrapers made of recycled materials touch the skies beside Vedic schools nestled in forests. Bullet trains run alongside bullock carts preserved as heritage. Sanskrit is not just a language of the past but the code of future AI interfaces, and the **Bhagavad**

Gita becomes a global leadership manual. This is the Bharat where inner peace meets outer progress, where diplomacy is led by compassion, and governance is inspired by sages.

In the heart of this utopia, lies the soul of the people—resilient yet gentle, diverse yet united. Bharat becomes the globe's moral compass, a living testament to the idea that a nation can be powerful without being oppressive, rich without being arrogant, and modern without being rootless. This *Swarga* is not in the heavens—it is being carved, breath by breath, by those who dare to dream and do.

This is the Bharat of **Chanakya 2050**. Not a perfect nation, but a purposeful one. Not a borrowed dream, but a ***Bharatiya Sankalp***—a solemn oath to build not just a country, but a **civilization reborn**.

Nuclear Realities: Global Threats, Treaties, and the Quest for Security in the Atomic Age

Since the first devastating use of nuclear weapons in 1945 on the Japanese cities of Hiroshima and Nagasaki, nuclear arms have remained among the most powerful and perilous tools of war ever created. Today, the world possesses approximately 13,000 nuclear warheads spread across nine countries: the United States, Russia, China, France, the United Kingdom, India, Pakistan, Israel (undeclared), and North Korea. Of these, Russia and the U.S. hold more than 90% of all warheads, with each maintaining thousands of weapons in active, reserve, and retired status. These weapons vary in design and purpose, primarily categorized as strategic nuclear weapons with long-range, high-yield destructive power; tactical nuclear weapons designed for battlefield use with lower yields; and the earlier generation atomic bombs based on fission reactions, largely replaced by thermonuclear fusion weapons with yields often measured in megatons. The presence of such weapons means that even a limited nuclear exchange could result in millions of deaths and catastrophic environmental damage globally.

The international community has long recognized the existential threat posed by nuclear arms and has developed several treaties to regulate their proliferation and use. **The Treaty on the Non-Proliferation of Nuclear Weapons (NPT)**, signed by 191 nations, stands as the cornerstone of these efforts. It seeks to prevent the spread of nuclear weapons, promote peaceful uses of nuclear energy under strict safeguards, and commit nuclear states to disarmament efforts. Despite its broad acceptance, the treaty is not without flaws, as key nuclear states such as India, Pakistan, and Israel remain outside its framework, and North Korea withdrew in 2003. The **Comprehensive Nuclear-Test-Ban Treaty (CTBT)** further prohibits all nuclear explosions but awaits entry into force, hindered by the failure of key states to ratify it. Bilateral arms control agreements, such as the **New START Treaty** between the United States and Russia, limit deployed strategic warheads to 1,550 each, though several other treaties have lapsed or been abandoned in recent years, raising concerns about a new arms race.

Complementing nuclear arms control are agreements banning other weapons of mass destruction. The **Biological Weapons Convention (BWC)** prohibits the development and stockpiling of biological warfare agents and counts over 180 signatories. The **Chemical Weapons Convention (CWC)** has overseen the destruction of over 98% of declared chemical weapons worldwide, enforcing norms against these devastating weapons. **Legal opinions, notably the 1996 advisory opinion of the International Court of Justice, affirm**

that the use or threat of nuclear weapons is generally incompatible with international humanitarian law due to their indiscriminate and disproportionate impact, yet political realities prevent a comprehensive ban.

Culturally, nuclear weapons have left an indelible mark on global consciousness. Films like *Dr. Strangelove* and *The Day After* illustrated the absurdity and horror of nuclear conflict, influencing public opinion and policy. Literature and art have reflected nuclear anxiety, with stories such as "On the Beach" and "Threads" portraying post-apocalyptic devastation to warn against nuclear war's catastrophic consequences. These cultural products have contributed to a global dialogue emphasizing the urgent need for disarmament and peace.

India's nuclear journey illustrates a unique blend of regional security concerns and a commitment to deterrence and responsible policy. Following its first "peaceful nuclear explosion" in 1974 and later weapon tests in 1998, India adopted a doctrine of credible minimum deterrence and a declared No First Use policy, pledging retaliation only if attacked by nuclear weapons. India's estimated arsenal of 160–170 warheads is complemented by a developing nuclear triad involving land-based missiles, air-launched weapons, and submarine-launched ballistic missiles, ensuring survivability and deterrence. Although outside the NPT, India actively engages in global non-proliferation and disarmament efforts, advocating for a fair, equitable international nuclear order.

Despite significant progress in arms reduction since the Cold War, modern challenges threaten global security. Nuclear modernization programs, emerging technologies such as hypersonic delivery systems, and geopolitical rivalries, particularly in South Asia and the Korean Peninsula, heighten risks. The potential for nuclear terrorism and accidental use adds complexity to the security environment. Effective protection against nuclear threats requires a multilayered approach, combining robust treaty frameworks, verification mechanisms like those enforced by the International Atomic Energy Agency, sustained diplomatic engagement, and public awareness.

The ongoing global quest for nuclear security rests on the shared recognition that while nuclear weapons may currently deter large-scale wars, their existence perpetuates a risk that humanity cannot afford. As new generations confront these challenges, the fusion of legal instruments, diplomatic efforts, cultural awareness, and technological safeguards will be essential to steer the world toward a safer, nuclear-weapons-free future.

The landscape of nuclear weapons and global security continues to evolve rapidly in the 21st century, shaped by new technological advancements, shifting geopolitical power balances, and emerging security challenges. Beyond the traditional nine nuclear-armed states, concerns have intensified over **nuclear proliferation risks linked to emerging technologies** such as cyber warfare and artificial intelligence, which could compromise command-and-control systems and increase the risk of accidental launches or unauthorized use. The integration of **hypersonic missiles**, capable of traveling at speeds exceeding Mach 5 and evading current missile defenses, introduces a new layer of strategic instability by compressing decision-making timelines for nuclear-armed states. Additionally, countries like **Iran and North Korea remain focal points of international efforts to curb nuclear development**, with Iran's controversial uranium enrichment program prompting renewed negotiations under the Joint Comprehensive Plan of Action (JCPOA) framework, while North Korea continues to test increasingly sophisticated ballistic missiles, claiming enhanced nuclear capabilities.

In terms of nuclear arms control, innovative diplomatic efforts are underway beyond traditional treaties. The **P5 (the five permanent members of the UN Security Council)**—China, France, Russia, the United Kingdom, and the United States—have periodically engaged in dialogues aimed at reducing the nuclear threat, though substantive disarmament progress has stalled in recent years. Meanwhile, the **Treaty on the Prohibition of Nuclear Weapons (TPNW)**, adopted by the United Nations in 2017, represents a landmark shift by legally banning nuclear weapons entirely for its 90+ state parties, reflecting a growing normative movement among non-nuclear states and civil society activists pushing for total abolition. This treaty, however, faces significant resistance from nuclear-armed states and their allies, who argue that deterrence remains essential to global security.

Another important aspect is the role of **nuclear energy and civilian nuclear programs** in the proliferation debate. The dual-use nature of nuclear technology—whereby civilian nuclear reactors can provide fissile material potentially usable in weapons—poses ongoing challenges for the **International Atomic Energy Agency (IAEA)**, tasked with inspection and verification to prevent diversion. Notably, India's **Civil Nuclear Agreement with the United States** in 2008 allowed it access to civilian nuclear technology and fuel despite not being a signatory to the NPT, recognizing India's responsible nuclear posture and opening doors for expanded nuclear energy cooperation globally.

The environmental and humanitarian consequences of nuclear weapons remain a critical concern. Studies estimate that even a **limited regional nuclear conflict**, for example between India and Pakistan involving 100 Hiroshima-sized weapons, could inject millions of tons of soot into the stratosphere, causing significant global cooling, drastic agricultural losses, and a potential "nuclear famine" threatening billions worldwide. This research underscores that nuclear war's catastrophic effects would extend far beyond the immediate blast zones, affecting global food security and ecosystems.

Finally, **nuclear deterrence doctrine itself faces scrutiny in an age of asymmetric warfare and emerging technologies**. The traditional logic of mutually assured destruction (MAD) is challenged by the rise of non-state actors, cyber threats, and space-based assets, leading to debates about the future relevance of nuclear arsenals. Some experts advocate for a shift toward new security architectures emphasizing arms control, conflict prevention, and disarmament verification technologies leveraging blockchain and AI to increase transparency and trust. As global powers recalibrate their strategic priorities, the international community stands at a crossroads—whether to renew commitments to reduce and eventually eliminate nuclear weapons or face heightened risks of proliferation and conflict in a rapidly changing world.

"Public Responsibility: The People's Mandate to Build the Nation"

The greatness of any nation is not solely determined by the brilliance of its leaders or the ambition of its policies, but by the day-to-day actions and mindset of its people. History testifies that public behavior has often been the invisible force shaping national destiny. Take the example of **Japan**, where a strong culture of self-discipline and responsibility is ingrained from early childhood—students clean their schools, follow civic rules meticulously, and treat public property with personal respect. This culture played a crucial role in Japan's post-World War II resurrection into a global economic powerhouse. In **Switzerland,** tax evasion is socially stigmatized, and 97% of adults file taxes honestly, enabling the state to provide high-quality public services with minimal corruption. In **South Korea**, public involvement in governance after the Korean War, particularly through educational commitment and a focus on technology, contributed to its transformation from poverty to prosperity in just a few decades. Even **Rwanda**, once synonymous with genocide, is today among Africa's cleanest and fastest-growing countries because of rigorous public discipline and monthly mandatory community work called ***Umuganda***. Citizens in such countries don't simply depend on their governments—they embody the government's vision through personal conduct. These are not isolated miracles but case studies in how **civic consciousness, when practiced by the masses, translates into national strength**.

Contrast this with India, where public responsibility often takes a backseat to public demands. According to the **Income Tax Department of India**, in FY 2022–23, only about **7.4 crore individuals** filed income tax returns out of a working population of over **60 crore**, indicating widespread tax evasion. A **2023 NITI Aayog study** estimated that over **62% of urban citizens** engage in some form of civic negligence—be it littering, encroachment, or vandalism. Despite the tireless efforts of campaigns like **Swachh Bharat Abhiyan**, a 2022 survey by the Quality Council of India found that **33% of public toilets in urban areas remained unusable** due to public misuse or neglect. Voter turnout, too, reflects a troubling trend—while rural India shows up in large numbers, **urban apathy** persists. The **2019 Lok Sabha**

elections saw **only 55% voter turnout in metro cities**, far below the national average. Ironically, the same population that complains about bad roads, waterlogging, and corruption often indulges in rule-breaking—bribing traffic cops, violating lane discipline, or vandalizing public infrastructure. The *"chalta hai"* attitude has not only normalized mediocrity but institutionalized it.

The solution lies not just in reforming politics but in **transforming public character**. To truly emerge as a **developed nation by 2047**, as envisioned in the Indian government's ***Amrit Kaal* roadmap**, Indian citizens must evolve from being passive consumers of governance to **active co-creators of national progress**. This means several things: first, embracing civic discipline—respecting traffic laws, cleanliness norms, and public property; second, exercising electoral rights responsibly—not just voting, but making informed choices and holding elected officials accountable; third, ensuring economic contribution by paying taxes and promoting ethical business practices; fourth, fostering community engagement through local problem-solving and neighborhood initiatives. The **Chanakya model of statecraft**, built on collective intelligence and citizen vigilance, can only be revived if every Indian acts not just as a beneficiary but as a custodian of democracy. Public participation in policymaking, such as through gram sabhas or digital platforms like *MyGov*, must become a norm, not an exception. The concept of **"Jan Bhagidari" (people's partnership)**, which was central to India's G20 Presidency theme in 2023, must move beyond diplomacy into everyday civic life.

If such changes take root, the transformation will be revolutionary. India can rise to become the **Vishwaguru**—not only in spiritual or cultural realms but in showcasing how **a**

billion people acting in civic unity can uplift an entire civilization. Economic indicators would improve as tax revenue increases; social harmony would deepen as citizens take ownership of mutual respect and responsibility; global perception would change as India becomes an example of people-led development. The **2022 UNDP Human Development Report** already noted India's digital public infrastructure as a model for the Global South—imagine its credibility when backed by equally responsible public behavior. India's cities could rival Singapore or Tokyo in cleanliness, traffic efficiency, and safety. Its democratic institutions could become stronger, faster, and more transparent with grassroots support.

But the consequences of public inaction are just as real. If citizens continue to ignore their duties, the price will be paid not in slogans, but in stalled reforms, deepening inequality, and moral decay. A democracy cannot survive on rights alone—it requires a balance of responsibilities. Without public initiative, **corruption will flourish, infrastructure will degrade, talent will migrate, and India will risk becoming a land of lost potential. It may still grow economically, but without civic dignity or moral leadership.** As **Sardar Vallabhbhai Patel** once warned, ***"Every citizen must remember that he is an Indian and he has every right in this country but with certain duties."*** The nation cannot be made great by government action alone. The path to **true development—*vikas*, not just growth—is paved not by policy, but by public conscience**. India's future will not be determined in Delhi alone, but in every home, street, school, and market across the country. The question is not just what the country is doing for its people, but **what the people are doing to deserve a greater country**.

New Era: AI as technological Advancement?

Artificial Intelligence (AI) is rapidly transforming the landscape of diplomacy and international relations. **According to a 2023 report by the World Economic Forum, over 70% of governments worldwide have adopted some form of AI-driven data analytics to inform policy decisions and diplomatic engagement.** AI systems excel at processing vast amounts of information—from satellite imagery and global news feeds to social media trends and economic indicators—at speeds impossible for human analysts. For example, **the United Nations has increasingly employed AI to monitor conflict zones, identify humanitarian crises, and track refugee movements in real time**, enabling quicker and more targeted diplomatic responses.

AI-powered natural language processing tools, including models like **ChatGPT developed by OpenAI,** have revolutionized communication by facilitating **instant translation, drafting diplomatic communiqués, and summarizing complex documents**. The European External Action Service (EEAS) has experimented with AI to scan and analyze foreign media for shifts in sentiment toward the European Union, allowing diplomats to anticipate changes in foreign policy or public opinion. Simulation software driven by AI helps negotiators visualize outcomes of potential agreements, providing a data-backed framework to support peace talks and conflict resolution.

Despite these breakthroughs, AI's role in diplomacy remains fundamentally **supportive rather than substitutive.** AI models such as ChatGPT, while powerful, lack consciousness, emotional intelligence, and the ability to understand cultural nuance—elements essential for effective diplomacy. For instance, the nuanced reading of a leader's tone during a speech or the historical context behind a nation's policy decision cannot be fully captured by AI algorithms. **Research from Stanford University highlights that even the most advanced AI struggles with "common sense reasoning"** and fails to grasp the implicit ethical and emotional underpinnings of human interactions, which are critical in trust-building and negotiation.

Moreover, AI systems are vulnerable to biases embedded in their training data. A **2022 study by MIT's Media Lab** demonstrated that many language models **reflect and sometimes amplify societal prejudices**, which, if unchecked, could distort diplomatic messaging or reinforce stereotypes. This is particularly dangerous in international relations, where misinterpretations can escalate tensions. Additionally, AI algorithms operate as **"black boxes"** with decision-making processes that are often opaque, raising concerns about accountability and transparency—qualities vital to diplomacy, where credibility and trust are paramount.

The security risks of AI in diplomacy are also significant. Autonomous weapons systems and AI-driven cyber-attacks pose novel threats to global peace and stability. The **Stockholm International Peace Research Institute (SIPRI)** reported in 2023 that more than a dozen countries have active programs developing AI-enabled military technologies, sparking fears of an arms race with destabilizing consequences. The possibility of AI being weaponized for misinformation campaigns or deepfakes threatens to undermine democratic processes and international trust.

Taking these facts into account, it is clear that AI—ChatGPT included—cannot replace the human element in diplomacy. Diplomacy requires empathy, ethical judgment, cultural sensitivity, and moral reasoning, none of which AI possesses.

Human diplomats interpret AI-generated data with wisdom, balancing quantitative insights against qualitative realities. For example, India's diplomatic corps often relies on a deep understanding of historical ties and cultural context that no AI can emulate. The final responsibility for decisions affecting peace, security, and cooperation must rest with humans who can appreciate the broader human consequences.

In conclusion, **while AI significantly enhances diplomatic tools and capacities, it remains just that: a tool. The irreplaceable human spirit**—characterized by empathy, intuition, and ethical conscience—**will always be central to diplomacy**. Ensuring that AI serves to complement rather than substitute human judgment will be critical to navigating the complexities of 21st-century international relations.

Building upon the transformative potential of AI in diplomacy, it is crucial to examine the challenges and limitations that underline the indispensable role of human agency. AI's rapid evolution has outpaced many international regulatory frameworks, creating a gap in governance that could destabilize diplomatic norms. According to the **United Nations Institute for Disarmament Research (UNIDIR)**, as of 2024, only a handful of countries have ratified comprehensive policies governing the use of AI in military and diplomatic applications, leaving much of the technology unregulated. This regulatory lag amplifies risks associated with misuse or accidental escalation—issues diplomats must manage with prudence and foresight.

Another challenge lies in the interpretability of AI outputs. Explainable AI (XAI) is a growing field aimed at making AI decisions more transparent, but current models remain complex and difficult to audit. For example, during the 2023 G20 summit, several participating countries expressed concerns over AI's opaque role in shaping policy advice, cautioning that unexamined reliance could lead to decisions that are not fully understood by human leaders or negotiators. This has reinforced the need for diplomats to retain final decision-making authority, ensuring that AI-generated insights undergo rigorous human scrutiny before action.

The geopolitical implications of AI deployment also underscore the irreplaceability of human diplomacy. AI-driven intelligence gathering can heighten surveillance capabilities, which in turn may provoke mistrust or retaliation between nations. **China and the United States, leading powers in AI development, have engaged in a cautious "AI diplomacy," balancing competition with cooperation on establishing ethical AI norms.** Human diplomats are vital in managing these delicate relationships, where technological advantage must be tempered with diplomatic engagement to prevent escalation or conflict.

Moreover, ethical considerations remain a core reason AI cannot replace humans. Unlike AI, diplomats engage with questions of justice, human rights, and humanitarian concerns—areas where moral reasoning and empathy are paramount. For instance, AI cannot weigh the human cost of sanctions or military interventions, nor can it advocate for vulnerable populations with genuine compassion. This is especially relevant in multilateral diplomacy, such as at the United Nations, where human values and political realities intersect in complex ways.

Finally, the future of AI in diplomacy must be envisioned as a partnership. AI tools will continue to evolve, with emerging capabilities like advanced predictive analytics, real-time translation, and automated monitoring becoming integral to diplomatic work. However, these tools must be wielded by skilled diplomats trained not only in international relations but also in ethical AI use and cyber security. The Indian Foreign Service, for example, has begun incorporating AI literacy into its training programs, recognizing the necessity of blending traditional diplomatic skills with technological savvy.

In sum, while AI represents a revolutionary asset in diplomacy's toolkit, it remains fundamentally a complement to—never a substitute for—the human touch. The essence of diplomacy lies in human creativity, emotional intelligence, ethical judgment, and the ability to foster trust and understanding among nations. As AI reshapes how information is gathered and analyzed, it is the unyielding human spirit that will ultimately safeguard peace, cooperation, and justice in the global arena.

AI may process facts, but only humans can deliver justice. Because some truths live beyond codes.

What it takes?

In the sacred rhythm of conch shells and monsoon rains, rises a dream as ancient as the Upanishads and as alive as the Indian soul—a vision of India as *Swarga*, not in the skies, but right here on Earth. This isn't mythology, it's a mission. A land where diplomacy becomes *dharma*, where politics bows to peace, and where governance is guided by grace. In this utopian India, the people are not ruled—they rise. No one sleeps hungry, no voice goes unheard, and no child grows up without hope. Harmony is not enforced, it flows—between religions, castes, tongues, and states. A Muslim calls a Hindu his brother, a Christian celebrates Diwali, a Sikh sings a Carnatic raga, and nobody looks twice—because difference is no longer danger, it is divine.

In this *Swarga*, justice doesn't come in delays or denials—it arrives like rain on dry soil. Courts speak truth, not jargon. Police protect, not persecute. Diplomats don't just defend borders—they defend the dignity of every Indian, anywhere in the world. Every citizen is a stakeholder in peace, every village a chapter of unity, every city a fusion of progress and tradition. Technology uplifts the poor, not alienates them. Temples feed the hungry, mosques shelter the lost, churches educate the forgotten. The streets are not arenas of survival, but of celebration. There is music in the markets, poetry in the parliaments, and laughter in every home.

Children grow up not fearing the world, but dreaming of it. Women walk without looking back. Youth create without migrating. Elders rest, not worry. Soldiers protect but never have to shoot. Borders exist, but they are silent, because diplomacy has turned neighbors into companions. Even nature breathes free—rivers are clean, skies are blue, tigers roam without threat, and trees outnumber towers.

This is the India imagined by the ancients, revived by the revolutionaries, and now—reborn through diplomacy. Not just a nation, but a *nirvana*. Not just a republic, but a sanctuary. This is the ultimate goal—not dominance, not development alone, but dignity for all. *Bharat as Swarga,* where peace is not a treaty—it's the air you breathe.

I truly believe that the road to lasting peace and prosperity for Bharat—and indeed for the world—lies not in vague ideals, but in *bold, uncompromising action*. Too often, peace is romanticized as a soft dream, a luxury for the privileged. But I ask—*how can peace be soft when it demands the hardest battles? The battle against injustice, apathy, and systemic violence?* I think peace requires strength, clarity, and fierce commitment.

One crucial lesson I insist upon is this: **equity must replace equality** as the foundation of every policy. Equality assumes everyone starts the race from the same line, but we know better—history, caste, class, and geography have stacked the deck for centuries. Should we pretend everyone has the same chance and call it fairness? Or should we design policies that lift those weighed down by generations of neglect, so they truly *thrive*? I choose the latter, because without equity, equality is just a mask for preserving privilege.

Skeptics will ask: *"But won't focusing on equity breed division? Isn't equality simpler and fairer?"* I counter: *Is it fair to hand a sword to someone fighting with bare hands and say, 'Good luck, you're equal now?'* True fairness means recognizing the battlefield and arming the vulnerable. Without equity, equality is an illusion, a lie dressed in statistics.

So how do we turn these principles into practice? First, by **redefining diplomacy as an act of human kindness, not just strategy**. India must lead the world by showing that power can be gentle and strength can be healing. What good is a nation feared for its weapons if it is forgotten for its compassion?

I envision a Bharat where foreign policy isn't just about borders and markets but about *people*—about refugees finding shelter, about youth from conflicting nations learning together, about climate accords that prioritize human survival over political posturing. Will critics say this is naive? I ask, '*Is it naive to imagine peace as a strategy for survival in a world teetering on conflict? Or is it madness to rely solely on force and fear?*'

On education, I firmly believe we must teach children to be *peacemakers* first—before technocrats, artists, or bureaucrats. The youth are not just the future voters but the future *voice* and *vanguard* of peace. Programs like **Model United Nations** and **Youth Parliaments** are not mere extracurricular activities; they are the **training grounds for tomorrow's diplomats and leaders** who will carry Bharat's soul forward. To those who dismiss these as fluff, I pose a question: *Is it better to invest in wars of the past, or in the peacemakers of tomorrow?*

Gender and social equity must be non-negotiable pillars. Women leading peace talks isn't a mere slogan—it is a proven formula for durable agreements. When marginalized communities rise to positions of influence, policies cease to be one-size-fits-all and start to *heal* historic wounds. If someone claims this breeds favoritism, I ask: *Is it favoritism to give a life jacket to someone drowning? Or is it survival?*

Technological advances must serve humanity's soul—not just its economy. In this age of AI and big data, I envision *"Digital Ahimsa"* where online spaces foster empathy rather than hate. Should we accept that technology only divides us? Or do we dare to build digital bridges?

Finally, the environment is the true foundation of peace. Without a planet that breathes freely, what is diplomacy but empty words? I advocate for *"Green Peace Zones"*—cross-border ecosystems that remind us that nature knows no politics, only coexistence. To cynics who see borders as walls, I ask: *What good is a wall if it chokes the air we all share?*

This vision is unapologetically idealistic, yet fiercely practical. It demands courage to question the status quo, to redefine power, and to place **human dignity at the center** of all we build. Because I think, in the end, peace is not passive. It is the **most active, revolutionary force** we possess.

If you ask me, *why fight so hard for peace?* I say, *because the alternative is a world where silence is broken only by sirens, where legacy is measured in rubble, and where future generations inherit fear instead of hope.*

Bharat's future is not to be a silent bystander but a luminous beacon—a nation where equity triumphs over mere equality, where power bows to compassion, and where peace is the fiercest victory of all.

Problems India needs to deal with:

1. Poverty

Poverty isn't just about empty pockets—it's about lost hope.

Solutions:

- Start more government-supported free meal programs (like mid-day meals) for the poor across all states.
- Provide skill-based training, not just free ration—so they can earn and live with dignity.
- Increase funding for self-help groups, especially in rural areas, so local women and youth can start earning through crafts, farming, etc.
- Addition of more job opportunities by government.

2. Unemployment

When a young person is jobless, the entire family suffers emotionally and financially.

Solutions:

- Start more skill and job training centres, especially in small towns and villages.
- Promote small businesses and startups with easy loans and less paperwork.
- Fix and speed up government job recruitment—delay breaks dreams.
- Promote local jobs over big degrees—dignity of labour should be respected.

3. Suicide Rates (Especially among Youth and Farmers)

No one wants to die—they just want someone to hear them.

Solutions:

- Make mental health support available and affordable in every district hospital.
- Train teachers and employers to notice mental stress signs early.
- Give farmers better crop prices, free insurance, and more direct support instead of just waivers.
- Reduce pressure of unrealistic expectations on students.

4. Cleanliness & Waste Management

Clean India is not just about picking up garbage—it's about national pride.

Solutions:

- Educate kids from a young age that cleanliness is patriotism.
- Put strict fines for public littering—and rewards for clean localities.
- Make sure every town and village has proper waste collection and recycling facilities.
- Encourage people to clean their own surroundings—not wait for the government.

5. High Prices (Inflation)

A normal family should not have to choose between food and medicines.

Solutions:

- Reduce unnecessary taxes on basic needs like food, LPG, and medicines.

- Support farmers directly to reduce middlemen and make things cheaper.
- Start ration shops with fair prices in every area.
- Encourage local produce and small vendors to grow and sell directly.

6. Corruption

Corruption doesn't start in big offices—it starts when people stay silent.

Solutions:

1. Digital systems for everything—from government tenders to job applications. No human, no bribe.
2. Protect and reward whistleblowers who expose corruption.
3. Rotate officers regularly so no one gets too powerful.
4. End the Donations System in colleges.

7. Justice System (Courts Delay)

Justice delayed is justice denied. Some people die waiting for their turn.

Solutions:

1. Increase the number of judges and courts.
2. Use fast-track courts for simple or old cases.
3. Introduce e-court hearings more widely—especially for rural areas.
4. Simplify the legal process so common people don't fear going to court.

5. Make it Compulsory for everyone to comprehend the basic legal framework of their nation.(In simple language by not making it complicated) which will help them to understand their own Fundamental Rights. After all, these rights are designed for them.

(Law is Meaningless if it cannot help the Common Man in the country.)

The Final Message

A Final Message from the Author: My Statement for Humanity

As I reach the final words of this journey, I don't write this as a scholar, a historian, or even an aspiring diplomat. I write this as a human being – deeply moved by the state of our world, and deeply hopeful for the kind of world we still have the power to shape. I write this with trembling honesty, because I believe we are living in an age that desperately needs more feeling, more listening, more healing.

I've always felt that Bharat – my beloved country – is not just a nation. It is a soul. A living, breathing spirit of compassion, resilience, and ancient wisdom that has withstood invasions, partitions, poverty, and prejudice, and still walks forward with open arms. And I think that's the Bharat the world needs to know – not just the rising power in the headlines, but the silent guardian of peace, the patient teacher of coexistence, the quiet warrior of love.

When I close my eyes and think of 2050, I don't see skyscrapers or GDP charts. I see a little girl in a village who has clean water, a boy in a refugee camp who has hope again, a student in Kashmir writing poetry instead of hearing gunshots, a farmer smiling at his harvest because he's finally respected. I see a world where peace isn't a summit we attend – but a language we live in.

I believe we've seen enough of hatred. We've built walls high enough. We've shouted across borders far too long. It's time to build bridges – not of steel, but of stories, of shared pain and common dreams. It's time we recognize that beneath every flag is a beating heart, and behind every enemy is a broken history that deserves healing. And I truly believe – with all my heart – that Bharat can lead this quiet revolution. Not with dominance, but with dignity. Not through might, but through meaning.

I don't want to live in a world where children know missiles before music. I don't want to raise a generation that thinks war is inevitable and kindness is naive. I want to live in a world where peace is not just possible – it is irresistible. And if my words can help even one person believe in that vision again, then I have done my part.

So here is my Vision – not as a writer, but as a soul among billions. Let us build a Bharat that is strong not because it can conquer, but because it can console. Let us build a world where diplomacy means listening before responding, where power means serving before ruling, where progress means saving lives – not just scaling economies.

I think the future doesn't belong to the richest or the loudest. It belongs to those who refuse to stop loving. And I believe Bharat – our Bharat – was born to love the world back to peace.

May we rise, not just as a power, but as a prayer for humanity.

– Mihir Bhagwat

Sources Used

1. Ministry of External Affairs (India)
2. United Nations (UN)
3. United Nations Development Programme (UNDP)
4. World Health Organization (WHO)
5. UNICEF
6. World Bank
7. International Monetary Fund (IMF)
8. World Trade Organization (WTO)
9. World Economic Forum (WEF)
10. United Nations Human Rights Council (UNHRC)
11. UNESCO
12. United Nations High Commissioner for Refugees (UNHCR)
13. International Court of Justice (ICJ)
14. International Criminal Court (ICC)
15. United Nations Security Council (UNSC)
16. G20 Summit – India Presidency 2023
17. World Inequality Report
18. NITI Aayog (India)
19. Lok Sabha and Rajya Sabha Debates Archives
20. National Crime Records Bureau (NCRB)
21. Ministry of Health and Family Welfare (India)

22. CoWIN Platform (India)
23. Vaccine Maitri Initiative (India)
24. Operation Ganga - MEA, Government of India
25. Digital India Programme
26. Aadhar & India Stack
27. Unified Payments Interface (UPI)
28. Indian Council of Medical Research (ICMR)
29. Press Information Bureau (PIB)
30. Ministry of Information and Broadcasting (India)
31. International Energy Agency (IEA)
32. Ministry of Environment, Forest and Climate Change (India)
33. Office of the High Commissioner for Human Rights (OHCHR)
34. Model United Nations India (MUN Circuit Reports)
35. Global Youth Trends Reports - UN & Commonwealth
36. IPCC (Intergovernmental Panel on Climate Change)
37. Global Soft Power Index - Brand Finance
38. National Statistical Office (NSO), India
39. Indian Council for Cultural Relations (ICCR)
40. Federation of Indian Chambers of Commerce & Industry (FICCI)
41. Observer Research Foundation (ORF)
42. Carnegie India
43. Brookings India
44. The Lancet - COVID India Case Studies
45. The Hindu / Indian Express / Hindustan Times
46. BBC, Al Jazeera, The Guardian

47. South Asia Terrorism Portal (SATP)
48. Stockholm International Peace Research Institute (SIPRI)
49. Asian Development Bank (ADB)
50. Pew Research Center
51. Gallup Global Attitudes Survey
52. Amnesty International Reports
53. Transparency International (Corruption Perception Index)
54. United Nations Office on Drugs and Crime (UNODC)
55. Global Youth Mobilization (UNICEF/WHO/YMCA)
56. Parliamentary Standing Committee Reports
57. Bollywood Industry Reports - FICCI-EY, KPMG
58. ICC (International Cricket Council) Reports
59. Indian Premier League (IPL) Annual Reports
60. National Education Policy (2020) - India
61. New Education and Digital Literacy Reports - UNESCO
62. World Happiness Report
63. Global Innovation Index
64. BharatNet & Digital Villages Programme
65. Startup India and Atal Innovation Mission (AIM)